50 U.S. STATES AND TERRITORIES

BY
MICHAEL KRAMME, Ph.D.

COPYRIGHT © 2000 Mark Twain Media, Inc.

ISBN   10-digit: 1-58037-140-X
          13-digit: 978-1-58037-140-7

Printing No. CD-1361

Mark Twain Media, Inc., Publishers
Distributed by Carson-Dellosa Publishing Company, Inc.

TABLE OF CONTENTS

INTRODUCTION

This book provides a resource for the study of the 50 states and the territories of the United States of America. Each chapter contains a one-page narrative about the state or territory. Each narrative includes facts of major importance or interest about the subject. An "at a glance" box contains basic statistics and information about each state. Also, each narrative contains an illustration of the state's or territory's flag.

Following each narrative is a short-answer question page. These questions provide a quick check of reading comprehension. Also included for each chapter is a geography exercise and suggestions for further reading or research.

Regional map exercises are included at the end of the book. These can be used as review exercises when the activities for all the states in a region have been completed.

Teachers may choose to use the readings as class projects or as extra enrichment activities for individual students. The activities lend themselves to individual student work. If the instructor would prefer to have group projects, he or she could organize the states by region, and the students could then enter into discussions of comparisons of the various states.

ALABAMA

The earliest inhabitants of what is now Alabama arrived over 11,000 years ago. Charcoal drawings made by these people still exist in Russell Cave.

During the sixteenth century, Spanish explorers, including Hernando de Soto, visited the area. They found many advanced Native American cultures. Tribes of Creek, Cherokee, Chickasaw, and Choctaw lived in the area at the time.

The French made the first permanent settlement on Mobile Bay in 1701. After the French and Indian War of 1763, the French lost the territory to the British. However, the Spanish continued to claim the southern part of the state. The British ruled until the land became the property of the United States. Alabama became the twenty-second state in 1819.

The Civil War had an important effect on Alabama. The state left the United States on January 11, 1861, and declared itself a republic. It then became one of the Confederate States of America. The state became known as the "Cradle of the Confederacy." Alabama's capital, Montgomery, was the first capital of the Confederacy. The state suffered throughout the war and the Reconstruction period that followed.

Helen Keller was one of the state's most noted citizens. She became blind and deaf as the result of a childhood illness. Through the work of her teacher, Annie Sullivan, she learned to communicate in spite of her disabilities. She became a noted author and a symbol of overcoming physical disadvantages.

One of Alabama's nicknames is the "Cotton State." Cotton was the major crop of the state for many years. However, an insect called the boll weevil almost wiped out the cotton crop at the beginning of the twentieth century. The town of Enterprise erected a monument to the boll weevil in 1919. The boll weevil disaster forced farmers to plant other crops, especially peanuts. An ex-slave, George Washington Carver, developed over 300 products and uses for the peanut alone.

The building of railroads and the establishment of a steel industry changed the economy of the state. Industries began to replace agriculture as the major source of income in the 1880s. Later industries included shipbuilding, chemicals, rubber, and mining.

Alabama was the location of many important civil rights events. On December 1, 1955, Rosa Parks refused to give her seat on a bus to a white passenger. Her act of defiance led to a Supreme Court ruling that bus segregation was unconstitutional. Martin Luther King, Jr., led the protest against her arrest. In 1965, Dr. King led a now-famous protest march from Selma to Montgomery.

Huntsville became an important part of the American rocket and space industry during the Second World War. American and German scientists worked together to develop rockets. The West launched its first satellite, *Explorer I,* in 1958. Both the satellite and its rocket were developed in Huntsville. The United States Space and Rocket Center is in Huntsville.

Capital: Montgomery
Nicknames: Heart of Dixie, Camellia State
Motto: We Dare Defend Our Rights
Major Cities: Birmingham, Mobile, Montgomery
Population: 4,352,000 (est.)
Area: 51,705 square miles, 29th largest
Major Industries: Agriculture, steel, chemicals, shipbuilding
Famous Citizens: George Washington Carver, Helen Keller
Flower: Camellia
Tree: Southern Pine
Bird: Yellowhammer

Name: _____   Date: _____

Questions for Consideration

1. What remains from the 11,000-year-old civilization in what is now Alabama?

    _____

2. What famous Spaniard explored the region?

    _____

3. Who made the first permanent settlement on Mobile Bay?

    _____

4. In what year did Alabama become a state?

    _____

5. What city was the first capital of the Confederacy?

    _____

6. Who was Helen Keller's teacher?

    _____

7. What insect almost wiped out Alabama's cotton crops?

    _____

8. Who developed over three hundred products and uses for the peanut?

    _____

9. Who refused to give up her seat on a bus?

    _____

10. What Alabama city became an important part of the American space industry?

    _____

Activities

Topics for special reports:

The Peanut
Cotton
George Washington Carver
Helen Keller
French and Indian War

Locate: On the map, put the number for each item in the proper location.

1. Florida
2. Georgia
3. Gulf of Mexico
4. Huntsville
5. Mississippi
6. Montgomery
7. Tennessee

ALASKA

Alaska comes from the Aleutian word meaning "great land." The name is appropriate. Alaska is the largest of all the states. It is one-fifth of the size of the entire United States. Alaska is twice the size of Texas, the nation's second-largest state.

Alaska's nickname is the "Last Frontier." It was the first state to be added to the union after a 47-year gap. It became a U.S. territory in 1912. The first bill to admit Alaska into the Union was proposed in 1917. However, it was not until 1959 that it became the forty-ninth state. Alaska still has vast unsettled regions. The population of Alaska is about one person for every square mile. It is the nation's most sparsely populated state.

Alaska has some unusual natural phenomena. In Fort Yukon, the temperature once reached 100°F. The record low of -80°F occurred at Prospect Creek. Alaska receives a large amount of snow. An average of 20 feet falls in parts of the state. Within one day, 74 inches fell at Mile 47 Camp.

The aurora borealis, or northern lights, appear from August through April. It is a beautiful display of a band of shimmering light.

Alaska is often called the "Land of the Midnight Sun." At Barrow, on the northern border, the sun shines continuously for 84 days from May 10 to August 2. However, there is no sunshine at Barrow for 67 days from November 18 to January 24.

Thousands of years ago, several aboriginal tribes crossed from Siberia over the Bering Strait into Alaska. These tribes were the ancestor tribes of the Aleut, Eskimo, Tsimshian, and Tlingit civilizations. A Danish explorer, hired by the Russian government, discovered the Bering Strait. Only a few miles separate Alaska from Russia at this point.

The Russians set up fur trading posts, but did not establish large settlements in the territory due to the harsh climate. The Russians sold Alaska to the United States for $7.2 million in 1867. The sale became known as Seward's Folly. William Seward, Abraham Lincoln's Secretary of State, made the treaty for the transaction. Many thought it was silly, or a folly, because they did not think it was worth the money.

Fishing and fur trading continued to be the major industries of Alaska until the discovery of gold. Prospectors discovered gold in Alaska in 1880. In 1896, a major gold rush began in the Klondike region of Canada. About 60,000 prospectors traveled through Alaska in search of gold. After the gold discoveries, mining and timber became of major importance. Oil and natural gas deposits added to the state's economy. Workers completed the Trans-Alaska pipeline in 1977. The pipeline provided a good method to move oil from the interior of the state to the port of Valdez.

Pollution is a potential problem for the oil industry. The tanker *Exxon Valdez* ran aground in Prince William Sound in 1989. It spilled over ten million gallons of oil into the water. This caused great damage to the wildlife and ecology of the region.

Capital: Juneau
Nicknames: Land of the Midnight Sun, The Last Frontier
Motto: North to the Future
Major Cities: Anchorage, Fairbanks, Juneau
Population: 614,000 (est.)
Area: 591,000 square miles, the largest state
Major Industries: Fishing, lumber, oil
Famous Citizen: William Egan
Flower: Forget-me-not
Tree: Sitka Spruce
Bird: Willow Ptarmigan

Name: _____ Date: _____

Questions for Consideration

1. What is the meaning of the Aleutian word *Alaska*?

   _____

2. How large is Alaska compared to Texas?

   _____

3. What are Alaska's nicknames?

   _____

4. What was the record low temperature recorded at Prospect Creek?

   _____

5. What is another name for the aurora borealis?

   _____

6. What was the nationality of the discoverer of the Bering Strait?

   _____

7. What nation sold Alaska to the United States?

   _____

8. When was gold discovered in Alaska?

   _____

9. In what year did Alaska become a state?

   _____

10. What was the name of the pipeline that was completed in 1977?

   _____

Activities

Topics for special reports:

Gold Rushes
Aurora Borealis
Eskimo

Locate: On the map, pu
for each item in the pro|

1. Anchorage
2. Barrow
3. Bering Strait
4. Canada
5. Fairbanks
6. Gulf of Alaska
7. Juneau

ARIZONA

One of several nicknames for Arizona is "the Grand Canyon State." The Grand Canyon is the state's most famous natural wonder. Over millions of years, the Colorado River has carved out the Grand Canyon. The canyon is about 217 miles long and up to 18 miles wide. It reaches a depth of one mile. In 1919, Congress created the Grand Canyon National Park.

The government built a series of dams to help tame the Colorado River and provide power. Major dams include the Boulder Dam (now named Hoover Dam), built in 1936, and the Glen Canyon Dam, finished in 1964.

Much of Arizona is desert. The temperature often exceeds 100°F. The highest recorded temperature was 127°F. Temperatures in the desert cool off significantly in the evenings. Temperatures often reach below zero in the mountain elevations.

Early inhabitants arrived in the region over 12,000 years ago. They carved homes out of the limestone mountains. Today, we refer to them as "cliff dwellers." Tribes of the Hopi, Yuma, Navajo, Apache, Pima, and Papago lived in the area when the first Europeans arrived. Today, Arizona has 23 Native American reservations. The tribes own over 20 million acres.

In 1536, Spanish explorers arrived looking for gold and other riches. They were the first Europeans to visit the area. In 1629, Spanish Franciscans established the first Catholic mission. When Mexico revolted against the Spanish government, the territory came under Mexican control in 1821. The United States gained control of most of Arizona after the Mexican-American War of 1846–1848. The U.S. government bought the rest of the state with the Gadsden Purchase of 1858.

The first copper mine opened in 1854, and the first gold mine opened two years later. Arizona soon became the nation's largest producer of copper.

Arizona experienced a large growth of population from the 1860s through the 1880s. Farmers and ranchers settled in the region, and the railroads arrived by the 1870s.

Many events of Wild West legend took place in Arizona. Geronimo and his men made several deadly raids in Arizona and Mexico. He finally surrendered in 1886. In 1888, Tombstone was the site of the famous gunfight at the O.K. Corral involving Wyatt Earp and Doc Holliday.

Arizona became the forty-eighth state on Valentine's Day of 1912.

Today, major crops are cotton, lettuce, and citrus fruits. Ranchers raise cattle, sheep, and hogs. Mining of copper, gold, and silver continues.

Water supply is a major concern for the state. The increased population, as well as agricultural and industrial needs, continues to demand more water.

The first dam for irrigation purposes was the Roosevelt Dam built in 1911 on the Salt River. The Hoover Dam also provides a major water supply. However, each year, Arizona uses much more water than can be replenished. The Central Arizona Project is currently under construction to help relieve the situation.

Capital: Phoenix
Nicknames: Grand Canyon State, Copper State
Motto: God Enriches
Major Cities: Phoenix, Tucson
Population: 4,669,000 (est.)
Area: 114,000 square miles, 6th largest
Major Industries: Agriculture, electronics
Famous Citizens: Barry Goldwater, Linda Ronstadt, Zane Grey
Flower: Saguaro Cactus Flower
Tree: Paloverde
Bird: Cactus Wren

Name: _____ Date: _____

Questions for Consideration

1. What is Arizona's most famous natural wonder?

   _____

2. What is the current name of Boulder Dam?

   _____

3. What was the highest temperature recorded in Arizona?

   _____

4. How many Native American reservations are in Arizona?

   _____

5. In 1821, what nation gained control over what is now Arizona?

   _____

6. Arizona is the nation's largest producer of what metal?

   _____

7. What famous Native American chief made several raids in Arizona?

   _____

8. What is the name of the most famous gunfight in Arizona's history?

   _____

9. On what day and year did Arizona become a state?

   _____

10. What is the name of the first dam built in Arizona for irrigation?

   _____

Activities

Topics for special reports:

Copper
Geronimo
The Grand Canyon
Hoover Dam
Mexican-American War
Wyatt Earp

Locate: On the map, put the number for each item in the proper location.

1. Colorado River
2. Mexico
3. New Mexico
4. Phoenix
5. Tucson
6. Utah

ARKANSAS

Arkansas has the only diamond mine in the United States. Diamonds were discovered in 1906. The mine operated from 1908 until 1925. It is now part of the Crater of Diamonds State Park. The park is the only place in America where visitors can keep any diamonds they find.

In addition to diamonds, bauxite was discovered in 1887, natural gas in 1909, and oil in 1919. Bauxite is a stone containing aluminum. Ninety-six percent of all bauxite mined in the United States comes from Arkansas.

Other interesting natural phenomena of the state are the hot springs. Native American tribes believed the springs were on holy land. The natives and later European settlers used the springs for relaxation and improving health. The area near the town of Hot Springs has 47 hot mineral springs.

Native tribes occupied the area for over 11,000 years before the coming of the Europeans. The Spaniard Hernando de Soto and his men visited the Mississippi Valley of the state in 1541. The Frenchmen Joliet and Marquette explored the region in 1673. La Salle claimed the territory for France in 1682. The French made the first permanent settlement, Arkansas Post, in 1686.

France lost the territory to Spain in 1762, but regained it in 1800. Arkansas was part of the Louisiana Purchase in 1803, and it became the twenty-fifth state in 1836.

On the eve of the Civil War, Arkansas voted to remain in the Union. However, after only two months, it seceded and joined the Confederacy. Major Civil War battles in the state included Pea Ridge and Prairie Grove. During part the Civil War, Arkansas had two capitals. The Union forces controlled the northern part of the state. Their capital was Little Rock. The Confederates controlled the southern part of the state. They established a capital in the town of Washington.

In September 1957, Governor Orval Faubus tried to stop nine African-American students from attending Little Rock's Central High School. This was in violation of a Supreme Court decision outlawing segregation. President Eisenhower called up federal troops to force the desegregation of the school.

The state capitol building in Little Rock is a one-quarter size replica of the nation's capitol.

Cotton was Arkansas's main crop throughout the nineteenth century. During much of the twentieth century, Arkansas remained one of the poorest states in the nation. The state government worked hard to bring industry into the state.

Arkansas is the home of the Welch Grape Juice Company. It also has many other major food-preparation industries. Food products are the largest part of the manufacturing segment of the economy. Arkansas also manufactures electrical equipment, metal products, and printed materials. The Wal-Mart Corporation began and maintains its headquarters in Benton.

In 1992, Arkansas native and former governor Bill Clinton became the forty-second President of the United States.

Capital: Little Rock
Nickname: Bear State, Wonder State
Motto: The People Rule
Major Cities: Little Rock, Fort Smith, Hot Springs
Population: 2,538,000 (est.)
Area: 53,187 square miles, 27th largest
Major Industry: Agriculture, electrical equipment, food products
Famous Citizens: William Clinton, "Dizzy" Dean, Glen Campbell
Flower: Apple Blossom
Tree: Pine
Bird: Mockingbird

Name: _____ Date: _____

Questions for Consideration

1. When were diamonds first discovered in Arkansas?

   _____

2. What element does bauxite contain?

   _____

3. How many hot mineral springs are near Hot Springs?

   _____

4. What European visited the region in 1541?

   _____

5. Who claimed the region for France?

   _____

6. What was the name of the first permanent settlement in Arkansas?

   _____

7. What was the name of the sale of the territory in 1803?

   _____

8. What were the two major Civil War battles in Arkansas?

   _____

9. What was the major crop of Arkansas in the nineteenth century?

   _____

10. What major company has its headquarters in Benton?

   _____

Activities

Topics for special reports:

Battle of Pea Ridge
President William Clinton
Diamonds
Hernando de Soto
Louisiana Purchase

Locate: On the map, put the number for each item in the proper location.

1. Benton
2. Hot Springs
3. Little Rock
4. Louisiana
5. Mississippi River
6. Missouri
7. Oklahoma

CALIFORNIA

California has the nation's largest population. It is the nation's third largest state. Only Alaska and Texas are larger.

California is a state of many contrasts. It has the nation's second highest peak, Mt. Whitney, at 14,494 feet. It also has the nation's lowest point, Death Valley, at 282 feet below sea level. The state's geography includes forests, deserts, mountain ranges, and fertile valleys. Yosemite Falls is the continent's highest waterfall. The world's oldest tree is over 4,600 years old. The world's tallest trees are the redwoods. One tree is 275 feet tall and over 100 feet around.

The state also has a diverse population. The minority population is over 43 percent. The population includes 25.8 percent Hispanic, 9.6 percent Asian-American, 7.4 percent African-American, and just under 1 percent Native American.

Native Americans lived in the California region for thousands of years. When the first Europeans arrived, natives spoke over 100 distinct dialects. In 1533, an expedition sent by Hernando Cortés first saw California. Cortés established a settlement two years later, but it was soon abandoned.

Sir Francis Drake claimed the northern part of the area for England in 1579. Several Spanish missionaries settled in the southern region beginning in 1769. The control of the area went from Spanish to Mexican in 1821. After the Mexican War, California came under the control of the United States.

The California gold rush began in 1848, when gold was discovered at Sutter's Mill. California became the nation's thirty-first state in 1850.

Settlers sailed around the tip of South America or came across prairie, desert, and mountains by wagon train to get to California. In 1869 the transcontinental railroad was completed, linking California with the rest of the nation. Settlers could now come by rail, and products could more easily be shipped to the East.

Capital: Sacramento
Nickname: Golden State
Motto: Eureka (I have found it)
Major Cities: Los Angeles, Sacramento, San Diego, San Francisco
Population: 32,667,000 (est.)
Area: 159,000 square miles, 3rd largest
Major Industries: Fruits, vegetables, motion pictures, computers, aerospace
Famous Citizens: Jack London, General Patton, Richard Nixon, Ronald Reagan, Shirley Temple
Flower: Golden Poppy
Tree: California Redwood
Bird: California Valley Quail

California experiences many earthquakes. The most famous one was in San Francisco in 1906. Other large earthquakes occurred in Los Angeles in 1971 and San Francisco and Oakland in 1989.

Three presidents had California connections. Herbert Hoover lived much of his life in the state. Ronald Reagan also lived much of his life there and served as the state's governor before becoming president. Yorba Linda was the birthplace of Richard Nixon. Nixon represented the state as a representative and senator in Congress before his election as vice president and president.

California is the nation's top manufacturing state. Major industries include electronics, electrical equipment, transportation equipment, food processing, printing, and motion pictures. It is also the leading state in farm income. Milk, beef, cotton, fruits, and vegetables are all major farm products.

Name: _____ Date: _____

Questions for Consideration

1. What is California's highest peak?

_____

2. Where is California's lowest point?

_____

3. What is California's highest waterfall?

_____

4. What are the world's tallest trees?

_____

5. What European first saw California?

_____

6. When did the California gold rush begin?

_____

7. Where was the gold discovered?

_____

8. When did California become a state?

_____

9. Where was California's most famous earthquake?

_____

10. Which U.S. president was born in California?

_____

Activities

Topics for special reports:

Death Valley
Earthquakes
Sir Francis Drake
Hernando Cortés

Locate: On the map, put the number for each item in the proper location.

1. Los Angeles
2. Mexico
3. Nevada
4. Pacific Ocean
5. San Diego
6. San Francisco
7. Sacramento

COLORADO

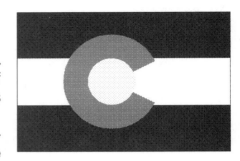

Colorado has the highest average altitude of any state. It has 54 mountains over 14,000 feet high. Twenty-seven of these are higher than Colorado's most famous mountain, Pike's Peak.

The nickname of Colorado's capital, Denver, is "the Mile-High City." The thirteenth step of the state capitol is exactly one mile above sea level.

The world's highest suspension bridge, the Royal Gorge bridge, crosses the Arkansas River.

Evidence exists that tribes of hunters roamed through Colorado about 20,000 years ago. About 100 B.C., basket-makers settled in the state. Later, both Pueblo and cliff-dwelling Anasazi tribes appeared in the state.

In 1888, a rancher discovered the cliff village at Mesa Verde. The city contained plazas and stone houses deserted for over 600 years. Some of the houses are two and three stories high. The Anasazi used ropes and ladders to climb from one story to the next.

By the time of the arrival of the Spaniards in the sixteenth century, Arapaho, Cheyenne, and Utes lived in the region.

Control of the region went back and forth between Spain and France until 1803. The Louisiana Purchase included part of Colorado. The rest of the state came under U.S. control after the Mexican War.

Colorado became the thirty-eighth state in 1876. One of its nicknames is the "Centennial State" since it became a state 100 years after the signing of the Declaration of Independence.

Early industries in the state included fur trade and agriculture. After their discovery, gold and silver mining became the most important influence in the state's history and economy.

Prospectors discovered gold in 1858 at Cherry Creek and in 1891 at Cripple Creek. A silver rush began in 1878. Leadville and Aspen became important silver mining towns. The most famous silver mine was the "Matchless Mine" owned by Horace Tabor. Other important discoveries included uranium in 1946 and shale oil in 1974.

Tourism is an important industry for Colorado. Colorado Springs became a popular health spa in the 1860s. Today it is the site of the U.S. Air Force Academy and the U.S. Olympic training facilities.

Rocky Mountain National Park, Mesa Verde National Park, and Dinosaur National Monument are popular tourist destinations. Aspen and Vail are two of the country's most popular ski resort areas.

The scenery in the state is spectacular. Katharine Lee Bates wrote the song "America the Beautiful" while visiting Pike's Peak in 1893.

In 1995, Colorado elected Ben Nightdress Campbell to serve in the U.S. Senate. Mr. Campbell was the first Native American to serve there.

Capital: Denver
Nickname: Centennial State
Motto: Nothing Without Providence
Major Cities: Colorado Springs, Denver, Pueblo
Population: 3,971,000 (est.)
Area: 104,000 square miles, 8th largest
Major Industries: Mining, tourism, scientific equipment
Famous Citizens: John Denver, Horace Tabor, Scott Hamilton
Flower: Rocky Mountain Columbine
Tree: Colorado Blue Spruce
Bird: Lark Bunting

Name: _____ Date: _____

Questions for Consideration

1. What is Colorado's most famous mountain?

   _____

2. What is the nickname of Colorado's capital, Denver?

   _____

3. What is the name of the world's highest suspension bridge?

   _____

4. What famous purchase included part of Colorado?

   _____

5. Where was gold first discovered in Colorado?

   _____

6. What was the name of Colorado's most famous silver mine?

   _____

7. What important discovery occurred in Colorado in 1946?

   _____

8. What area of Colorado became a popular health spa just before the Civil War?

   _____

9. What are two popular ski resort areas in Colorado?

   _____

10. What famous song was written while the composer visited Colorado in 1893?

    _____

Activities

Topics for special reports:

Zebulon Pike
Lead
Mesa Verde
Rocky Mountains
Silver

Locate: On the map, put the number for each item in the proper location.

1. Aspen
2. Colorado Springs
3. Denver
4. Leadville
5. Pike's Peak
6. Pueblo

CONNECTICUT

Some of the Puritans who settled in Massachusetts were unhappy with their government, so they resettled in what is now Connecticut. They wrote a set of laws in 1639. The set of laws, named the Fundamental Orders, was the first constitution in the New World. The colonial laws became one of the sources for the U.S. Constitution. One of Connecticut's nicknames is the "Constitution State."

King Charles II of England gave a charter to Connecticut that gave the colony several rights. The Royal Governor of New York demanded the colonists give the charter to him. Instead, they hid the charter in a hollow oak tree. The tree became a landmark known as the Charter Oak.

Connecticut supplied many troops with guns and gunpowder during the Revolutionary War. The state became known as the "arsenal of the nation." Many noted Revolutionary War persons were from Connecticut, including Nathan Hale, Ethan Allen, and Benedict Arnold. Hale became a spy for the colonists. Just before the British hanged him, he said, "I regret that I have but one life to lose for my country." Arnold turned against the colonists and aided the British. He became the most famous traitor in our nation's history.

Connecticut became the fifth state to ratify the Constitution.

The southern border of the state is on Long Island Sound. The sound connects directly with the Atlantic Ocean. Connecticut became an important sailing center. Ships from Connecticut sailed throughout the world. Today, Mystic Seaport is a living museum. It has a recreated whaling village, the whaling ship *Charles Morgan*, and an aquarium.

The government established the first submarine station at Groton in 1917. Workers launched the first atomic submarine, the USS *Nautilus*, in Groton in 1954.

Capital: Hartford

Nicknames: Constitution State, Nutmeg State

Motto: He Who Transplanted Still Sustains

Major Cities: Hartford, Bridgeport, New Haven

Population: 3,274,000 (est.)

Area: 5,000 square miles, 48th largest

Major Industries: Defense equipment, insurance

Famous Citizens: Ethan Allen, Benedict Arnold, Noah Webster, P.T. Barnum, Mark Twain, Harriet Beecher Stowe

Flower: Mountain Laurel

Tree: White Oak

Bird: American Robin

Two of America's greatest writers were neighbors. Harriet Beecher Stowe and Mark Twain lived on the same block in Hartford. Stowe was the author of the famous book *Uncle Tom's Cabin*. Twain's most famous books were *The Adventures of Tom Sawyer* and *The Adventures of Huckleberry Finn*. He also wrote *A Connecticut Yankee in King Arthur's Court*.

Connecticut continued as a manufacturing center. It became a major producer of machine tools, typewriters, silverware, hats, and electronic equipment. It continued to be a provider of defense items. During the Civil War, Colt and Winchester produced arms for the Union Army. The state supplied weapons during both world wars. Today, its factories continue making ammunition, airplane engines, shell cases, helicopters, and submarines.

The first organized insurance company began in Hartford. It wrote its first policy in 1794. Today Hartford continues as a major insurance center, and is the base of 45 insurance companies.

Name: _____ Date: _____

Questions for Consideration

1. What was the first constitution in the New World?

   _____

2. Who gave the charter to Connecticut?

   _____

3. Where did the colonists hide the charter?

   _____

4. What was Nathan Hale's famous quote?

   _____

5. What is Benedict Arnold known as today?

   _____

6. What living museum with a recreated whaling village is in Connecticut?

   _____

7. What was the name of the first atomic submarine?

   _____

8. Who wrote *Uncle Tom's Cabin*?

   _____

9. Who produced arms for the Union Army?

   _____

10. For what industry is Hartford known?

   _____

Activities

Topics for special reports:

Benedict Arnold
Nathan Hale
Insurance
Harriet Beecher Stowe
Whaling

Locate: On the map, put the number for each item in the proper location.

1. Bridgeport
2. Hartford
3. Long Island Sound
4. Massachusetts
5. New York
6. Rhode Island

DELAWARE

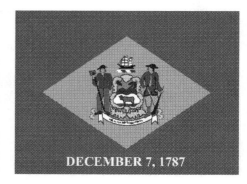

DECEMBER 7, 1787

Sailing for the Dutch, the English explorer Henry Hudson sailed into Delaware Bay in 1609. At that time, the Lenni Lenape (now known as the Delaware) and the Nanticoke tribes dominated the region.

The region received its name in 1610. A storm blew a ship sailing from Virginia to England off course. The ship's captain found safety in a bay. He named the bay and land after the Governor of Virginia, Lord de la War.

By 1631, the Dutch, under the leadership of Peter Minuit, built the settlement of Zwaanendael. Native Americans destroyed the settlement just one year later. The Dutch resettled in 1651 near New Castle.

The Swedes established their first settlement in the state in 1638. They named their settlement Fort Christina in honor of the Queen of Sweden. The site of Fort Christina is the present location of Wilmington. The region around the fort became known as New Sweden.

The Swedish pioneers of Delaware built the first log cabins in North America. The design using split logs was similar to those built in their homeland. The Dutch, led by Peter Stuyvesant, defeated the Swedes in 1655. However, the Dutch allowed them to keep their property.

The British took control of the region in 1664. The British ceded the land to William Penn in 1682, and Delaware became part of Pennsylvania. Delaware had its own elected government in 1704, but was still part of Pennsylvania. It gained its independence in 1776.

During the Revolutionary War, one of the state's militia fought under the name of the Blue Hen's Chickens. The name came from the pet chicken of the unit's captain.

During the Declaration of Independence debates, Caesar Rodney was one of Delaware's representatives. He was quite ill and had to return home to Dover. He insisted that he be brought back to vote. He rode through the night in spite of his illness to sign the Declaration. The reverse side of the quarter honoring Delaware, minted in 1999, honors Rodney's famous ride. He also voted for ratification of the Constitution on December 7, 1787, allowing Delaware to be the first state in the Union to ratify the Constitution. Today, its nickname is "the First State."

Capital: Dover
Nickname: The First State
Motto: Liberty and Independence
Major Cities: Dover, Wilmington
Population: 744,000 (est.)
Area: 2,000 square miles, 49th largest
Major Industry: Chemicals
Famous Citizens: Ceasar Rodney, the Du Pont family
Flower: Peach Blossom
Tree: American Holly
Bird: Blue Hen Chicken

During the Civil War, Delaware was still a slave state, but it did not secede from the Union. Delaware did not abolish slavery until the adoption of the thirteenth amendment in 1865.

The first major industry in Delaware began in 1802. The Du Pont family began manufacturing gunpowder. The Du Pont company continues to be a major part of the nation's chemical industry.

Railroads and several canals brought many other industries into the state. Delaware became home to several mills, shipyards, and foundries.

Near the end of the nineteenth century, the state legislature passed a tax law that gave advantages to corporations. Delaware soon became the home of many corporate headquarters.

Name: _____ Date: _____

Questions for Consideration

1. Who discovered Delaware in 1609?

    _____

2. For whom was Delaware named?

    _____

3. Who led the first Dutch settlement in Delaware?

    _____

4. Who built the first log cabins in North America?

    _____

5. What territory included Delaware from 1682 until 1776?

    _____

6. What was the nickname of Delaware's militia during the Revolutionary War?

    _____

7. Who signed the Declaration of Independence for Delaware?

    _____

8. What did the Du Pont family first manufacture in Delaware?

    _____

9. What industry is the Du Pont company noted for today?

    _____

10. Why did Delaware become the home of many corporate headquarters?

    _____

Activities

Topics for special reports:

Corporations
Declaration of
    Independence
Gunpowder
Henry Hudson

Locate: On the map, put the number for each item in the proper location.

1. Atlantic Ocean
2. Dover
3. Maryland
4. Pennsylvania
5. Wilmington

FLORIDA

Explorer Juan Ponce de León named the region *Florida,* a Spanish word meaning "many or full of flowers."

Florida has many nicknames, all of them appropriate. It is the "Sunshine State" due to the large number of sunny days there. It is the "Peninsula State" since it is surrounded on three sides by water. It is the "Orange State" due to its citrus industry. Another nickname is the "Everglade State" for its famous swamp, and it is called the "Alligator State" for the swamp's most noted inhabitants.

Ponce de León visited the region in 1513 looking for the fountain of youth. He claimed the area for Spain. He returned to establish a settlement in 1521, but was killed by the natives. Hernando de Soto explored the area near Tampa Bay in 1539.

Some French settlers established a colony in 1564, but were soon conquered by the Spanish. The Spanish established St. Augustine in 1565. St. Augustine is the oldest city in the United States.

Spain traded Florida to the British for Cuba. During the Revolutionary War, the settlers remained loyal to Britain. The Spanish regained the territory in 1783 and then gave control of it to the United States in 1819.

A war between the Seminole Native Americans and the United States raged from 1835 to 1842. The United States forced the Seminoles out of the territory. The Seminoles never officially signed a treaty, so technically they are still at war with the U.S. government.

Florida became the twenty-seventh state in 1845. It joined the Confederacy in 1861 and was readmitted to the Union in 1868.

Florida became a major part of the U.S. space program when it launched its first rocket from the Cape Canaveral Space Center. The government later changed the name of the facility to the Kennedy Space Center. Most of the space launches of major importance occur there. The John Glenn flight, the *Apollo 11* Moon mission, and the *Columbia* Space Shuttle mission all began at the Kennedy Space Center.

Florida's first industry was cotton. Later the citrus industry and agriculture became of primary importance. Florida is the nation's largest supplier of orange juice.

Tourism became a major industry at the beginning of the twentieth century. Florida is the home of many major tourist attractions. The largest attraction is the Disney complex of Disney World, Epcot Center, Disney-MGM Studios, and Animal Kingdom. Other major tourist sites include Busch Gardens, Cypress Gardens, Daytona Beach Speedway, Everglades National Park, Sea World, and Universal Studios.

Florida experiences many hurricanes. One of the most devastating was Hurricane Andrew, which struck in 1992. It killed 38 people and caused over 20 billion dollars in damage.

Capital: Tallahassee
Nickname: Sunshine State
Motto: In God We Trust
Major Cities: Tallahassee, Miami, Orlando, Tampa
Population: 14,916,000 (est.)
Area: 59,000 square miles, 22nd largest
Major Industries: Tourism, citrus fruits
Famous Citizens: Charles and John Ringling, Marjorie Kinnan Rawlings, Osceola, Faye Dunaway, Sidney Poitier
Flower: Orange Blossom
Tree: Sabal Palmetto Palm
Bird: Mockingbird

Name: _____ Date: _____

Questions for Consideration

1. Who named Florida?

   _____

2. Why is one of Florida's nicknames "the Peninsula State"?

   _____

3. What is the name of Florida's most famous swamp?

   _____

4. What is the oldest city in the United States?

   _____

5. When did the United States get final control of Florida?

   _____

6. What Native American tribe is still officially at war with the United States?

   _____

7. What was the original name of the major space center in Florida?

   _____

8. Of what fruit juice is Florida the major producer?

   _____

9. What is the largest tourist attraction in Florida?

   _____

10. What was the name of the devastating hurricane that hit Florida in 1992?

   _____

Activities

Topics for special reports:

The Everglades
Hurricanes
Kennedy Space Center
Juan Ponce de Leon
Oranges

Locate: On the map, put the number for each item in the proper location.

1. Atlantic Ocean
2. Gulf of Mexico
3. Miami
4. Orlando
5. Tallahassee
6. Tampa

GEORGIA

Spanish explorer Hernando de Soto was the first European to explore what is now Georgia. Some French Huguenots settled there in 1562, but left after just a few years. The Spanish then established several missions along the Atlantic Coast. They left the missions after several attacks by Native Americans, pirates, and the British. The British soon gained control of the region from the Spanish.

King George II of England granted a charter to James Edward Oglethorpe to establish a settlement in the new territory. The settlement became known as Savannah. Oglethorpe named the territory Georgia in honor of King George. Much of Georgia remained under British control during the Revolutionary War. The British surrendered control of Savannah in 1782. Six years later, Georgia became the fourth state to ratify the Constitution.

Conflicts arose with the Creek and Cherokee Native American tribes as European settlers moved into the state. Settlers forced the Creeks out of the state by the late 1820s. The conflicts increased with the discovery of gold in 1827. The government set up a mint and manufactured gold coins in Dahlonega from 1838 until 1861.

In 1838, the U.S. government forced the Cherokees to walk from Georgia to reservations in Oklahoma. Thousands of Cherokees died during the walk. This forced migration became known as "The Trail of Tears."

Georgia left the Union to join the Confederacy in 1861. During the Civil War, Georgia suffered more destruction than any other state. General Sherman's famous "March to the Sea" cut a path of damage from Atlanta to the Atlantic Ocean. Georgia remained under military rule until it was readmitted to the Union in 1870.

Cotton was Georgia's major industry for many years, but the boll weevil destroyed most of the crop in 1921. After the boll weevil disaster, the state broadened its economy. Today, major industries include poultry, textiles (especially carpet), transportation equipment, and paper.

Atlanta became the state's capital in 1868. It is one of the South's largest and fastest-growing cities. Atlanta's airport is the second-busiest in the nation. Atlanta hosted the 1996 Summer Olympic Games. The Martin Luther King, Jr., Historic Site and the Carter Presidential Library are located in Atlanta.

Native Americans discovered and used hot mineral springs in the western part of the state. By the late 1800s, a major resort and spa industry began. President Franklin D. Roosevelt began visiting a spa near the town of Warm Springs. The soothing waters helped with his treatments for polio. Roosevelt built a small house there and used it as a second home. Roosevelt died there on April 12, 1945. His Warm Springs home is now open to visitors.

Plains, Georgia, is the birthplace of James Earl (Jimmy) Carter, Jr., the United States's thirty-ninth president.

Georgia is also the birthplace of Dr. Martin Luther King, Jr. King began his civil rights work in Georgia.

Capital: Atlanta
Nickname: Peach State
Motto: Wisdom, Justice, and Moderation
Major Cities: Atlanta, Savannah
Population: 7,642,000 (est.)
Area: 59,000 square miles, 21st largest
Major Industries: Agriculture, textiles
Famous Citizens: Jimmy Carter, Ted Turner, Ray Charles
Flower: Cherokee Rose
Tree: Live Oak
Bird: Brown Thrasher

Name: _____ Date: _____

Questions for Consideration

1. Who first explored Georgia?

   _____

2. For whom was Georgia named?

   _____

3. What Georgia city was once the site of a U.S. Mint?

   _____

4. What is the name of the forced move of the Cherokees out of Georgia?

   _____

5. In what year did Georgia join the Confederacy?

   _____

6. What insect changed Georgia's economy?

   _____

7. What city hosted the 1996 Olympics?

   _____

8. Which president built a home at Warm Springs?

   _____

9. Which president was born in Georgia?

   _____

10. What noted civil rights leader was born in Georgia?

   _____

Activities

Topics for special reports:

James Earl Carter, Jr.
Cherokee Native Americans
Sherman's March to the Sea
Dr. Martin Luther King, Jr.
Peaches

Locate: On the map, put the number for each item in the proper location.

1. Alabama
2. Atlanta
3. Atlantic Ocean
4. Florida
5. Savannah
6. South Carolina

HAWAII

Hawaii's nickname is "the Aloha State." *Aloha* is the native word meaning "love." Hawaiians use it as a greeting for hello, good-bye, welcome, or farewell.

Hawaii is the only state that is entirely made up of islands. About 135 islands make up the state. The islands are actually the peaks of volcanoes rising from the floor of the Pacific Ocean. The volcanoes formed the islands over 25 million years ago.

About 80 percent of the people of Hawaii live on the island of Oahu. The other larger islands include Hawaii, Maui, Lanai, Molokai, Niihau, and Kauai.

Hawaii is also the only state that was once an independent monarchy. Eight kings and queens ruled from 1795 until 1893. King Kamehameha I gained control over and united the islands. His grandson, King Kamehameha III, gave his nation its first written constitution. He based it on many government ideas of the Western nations. The last ruler of the island was Queen Liliuokalani. American business interests caused the overthrow of her government in 1893.

The first people to live on the islands were Polynesians who arrived in large canoes around A.D. 400. The trip was over 2,000 miles long. Others from Tahiti arrived a few centuries later. Hawaii continued to be a "melting pot" with the arrival of large numbers of Chinese, Japanese, Filipinos, Koreans, and Americans.

In 1778, Captain James Cook was the first European to visit the islands. He named them the Sandwich Islands in honor of his patron, the Earl of Sandwich. Cook returned to the islands the following year and was killed by the natives.

Missionaries from the United States arrived in the early 1800s. They established newspapers, churches, and public schools. Unfortunately, they also brought diseases to the island for which the natives had little resistance. Over half the native population died from these diseases.

The increased presence of U.S. citizens and businesses led to annexation by the United States in 1898. Two years later, Hawaii became a U.S. territory. Hawaii became the fiftieth state in 1959.

Capital: Honolulu

Nickname: Aloha State

Motto: The Life of the Land is Perpetuated in Righteousness

Major Cities: Honolulu, Hilo, Kailua

Population: 1,193,000 (est.)

Area: 6,000 square miles, 47th largest

Major Industries: Tourism, agriculture

Famous Citizens: Queen Liliuokalani, Sanford B. Dole, Bette Midler

Flower: Hibiscus

Tree: Kukui (Candlenut)

Bird: Nene (Hawaiian Goose)

Hawaii is the site of Pearl Harbor. On December 7, 1941, the Japanese attacked a U.S. navy base located there. The attack destroyed over 18 warships, 200 airplanes, and cost over 4,400 lives. The attack led to the entrance of the United States into World War II.

Tourism is a major industry of Hawaii. It is famous for its beautiful scenery and beaches. Favorite destinations include Hawaii Volcanoes National Park, the USS *Arizona* Memorial at Pearl Harbor, Hulihee and Iolani Palaces, and the Waikiki resort area.

Early industries of Hawaii included sandalwood and whaling. Both sugar cane and pineapple became major crops in the nineteenth century. Sugar and pineapple still dominate Hawaii's exports.

Hawaii suffered a devastating hurricane, Iniki, in 1992, which caused over $1.4 billion in damages.

Name: _____ Date: _____

Questions for Consideration

1. What is Hawaii's nickname?

   _____

2. How many islands make up Hawaii?

   _____

3. On which island do most of the people of Hawaii live?

   _____

4. How many kings and queens have ruled Hawaii?

   _____

5. Who were the first people to live on the islands?

   _____

6. Who was the first European to visit Hawaii?

   _____

7. In what year did Hawaii become the fiftieth state?

   _____

8. What historic event happened on December 7, 1941?

   _____

9. What memorial is located at Pearl Harbor?

   _____

10. What are Hawaii's two major crops?

   _____

Activities

Topics for special reports:

Captain James Cook
Pearl Harbor
Pineapples
Queen Liliuokalani
Sugar Cane
Volcanoes

Locate: On the map, put the number for each item in the proper location.

1. Hawaii (the island)
2. Honolulu
3. Kailua
4. Kauai
5. Maui
6. Oahu

IDAHO

When most people think of Idaho, they think of potatoes. Idaho's farmers grow more potatoes than any other state. Over 25 percent of the nation's potatoes come from Idaho. Other crops grown in the state include sugar beets, alfalfa, bluegrass seed, and hops. Idaho also has large cattle and timber industries.

Idaho has many artifacts of its ancient people including examples of cave and cliff writings and drawings. The largest preserved prehistoric drawing in the nation is near the Snake River.

Six major tribes lived in the region when the first Europeans arrived. Members of the Shoshone, Paiute, Kutenai, Coeur d'Alene, and Nez Perce tribes lived throughout the state.

Much of Idaho was part of the Louisiana Purchase of 1803. The first white men to enter Idaho were the members of the Lewis and Clark expedition. The expedition, sent by President Thomas Jefferson to explore the lands of the Louisiana Purchase, entered the state in August 1805. The Nez Perce Native Americans aided the expedition by providing food, canoes, and guides.

The first Europeans to live in the territory were fur traders. The North West Fur Company built a trading post in 1809. By 1840, the Hudson's Bay Company controlled most of the region.

Missionaries arrived in the 1830s, and Henry Spalding established a mission among the Nez Perce in 1836. As more whites moved into the region, a series of conflicts with the natives began. The Nez Perce War continued until the signing of a treaty in 1872.

The United States gained control of the Pacific Northwest region, including the portion of Idaho not included in the Louisiana Purchase, from Britain in 1846.

The opening of the Oregon Trail increased traffic through the state. Over 500,000 Americans traveled along the trail. Most of the people traveled through the state rather than settled there. Many began to stay after the discovery of gold, however, and Idaho became a territory in 1863 and the forty-third state in 1890.

One of Idaho's many nicknames is "the Gem State." Numerous discoveries of gems and precious metals led to this name. Major discoveries included gold in 1860 and silver in 1880. Gem stones found in the state include diamonds, rubies, sapphires, agates, aquamarines, beryl, opals, and topaz.

Idaho contains many natural wonders. It has 42 mountains over 10,000 feet high. It is a major recreational region. Idaho has over 3,200 miles of white water rivers, more than any other state. Popular activities include boating, fishing, hunting, skiing, and camping. It is the location of 11 national forests, parks, and recreational areas. The most famous of these include part of Yellowstone National Park, Craters of the Moon National Park, and Hell's Canyon National Recreation Area. Idaho also contains a large number of state parks and recreation areas for both summer and winter activities.

Capital: Boise
Nickname: Gem State
Motto: It is Perpetual
Major Cities: Boise, Idaho Falls, Pocatello
Population: 1,229,000 (est.)
Area: 84,000 square miles, 13th largest
Major Industry: Agriculture
Famous Citizens: Ezra Pound, Lana Turner, Chief Joseph, Sacajawea
Flower: Syringa
Tree: Western White Pine
Bird: Mountain Bluebird

Name: _____ Date: _____

Questions for Consideration

1. What is Idaho's most famous crop?

_____

2. Near what river is the largest preserved prehistoric drawing in the United States?

_____

3. Who were the first whites to enter the territory?

_____

4. Which Native American tribe helped the first white explorers?

_____

5. What was the occupation of the first European settlers in Idaho?

_____

6. What famous trail brought over 500,000 Americans through Idaho?

_____

7. Which of Idaho's nicknames is given in the narrative?

_____

8. How many mountains over 10,000 feet high are in Idaho?

_____

9. How many miles of white water rivers travel through Idaho?

_____

10. How many national forests, parks, and recreational areas are in Idaho?

_____

Activities

Topics for special reports:

Fur Trading
Lewis and Clark
    Expedition
Nez Perce
Oregon Trail
Potatoes

Locate: On the map, put the number for each item in the proper location.

1. Boise
2. Canada
3. Montana
4. Oregon
5. Pocatello
6. Washington

ILLINOIS

Abraham Lincoln is Illinois' most famous citizen. Though he was born in Kentucky and grew up in Indiana, he spent most of his life in Illinois. Visitors can see the reconstructed village of New Salem where Lincoln spent part of his youth. Other Lincoln sites include his home and tomb in Springfield.

Other presidents to have Illinois connections include Ulysses S. Grant and Ronald Reagan. Grant lived in Galena both before and after the Civil War. Reagan was born in Tampico.

Illinois received its name from the Illini Native Americans. The Illini were six tribes joined together in the 1500s. The first inhabitants came to the region thousands of years before the Illini. Between 300 B.C. and A.D. 500, the Hopewells lived in the Midwest. Later, the Middle Mississippians appeared. Both were mound builders. They built mounds for burials. Over 10,000 mounds remain in the state. Visitors may see examples of these mounds at the Dixon Mounds State Museum and the Cahokia Mounds State Historic Site.

The first whites to see the state were Louis Joliet and Jacques Marquette in 1673. The French established a mission and a fort within the next few years. The French established the first permanent white settlement in 1699. The French turned control over to the British in 1765. The British lost control to the United States during the Revolutionary War. Illinois became the twenty-first state in 1818.

The first settlers were mainly farmers. With the building of railroads and a canal system, the state became a major industrial and commercial center.

Springfield is the capital of Illinois. However, Chicago is the largest city in the state and the third largest in the nation. Chicago became a major commercial center for the Midwest with the opening of the Erie Canal. The canal allowed goods to be shipped easily from Chicago to the east coast and Europe.

Chicago suffered a devastating fire in 1871. The fire destroyed much of the city and killed over 300 people. The city rebuilt immediately.

Capital: Springfield
Nicknames: Prairie State, Land of Lincoln
Motto: State Sovereignty, National Union
Major Cities: Chicago, Springfield
Population: 12,045,000 (est.)
Area: 56,000 square miles, 24th largest
Major Industries: Agriculture, machinery
Famous Citizens: Abraham Lincoln, Frank Lloyd Wright
Flower: Native Violet
Tree: White Oak
Bird: Cardinal

Chicago was the home of the first skyscraper. Built in 1884, it was a ten-story building using steel beams to support the walls. Today, Chicago is the site of one of the world's tallest buildings, the 110-story Sears Tower.

Chicago hosted the 1893 World's Fair. It commemorated the four-hundredth anniversary of Columbus's voyage. They planned to open the fair on the 1492 anniversary, but the building of the fair took longer. Many visitors to the fair took their first ride on a Ferris wheel. They also saw the latest technology, including the new electric light.

From the time of its early settlement, Illinois was a major agriculture center. Today, it continues to produce large quantities of corn, soybeans, cattle, and hogs. By the 1880s, Illinois became a major producer of steel, and a leader in meat packing, banking, and transportation. Illinois continues to be a leading industrial state today.

Name: _____ Date: _____

Questions for Consideration

1. In what village did Abraham Lincoln spend part of his youth?

   _____

2. Which president was born in Illinois?

   _____

3. Who were the first whites to see Illinois?

   _____

4. How many Native American mounds still exist in Illinois?

   _____

5. When did Illinois become a state?

   _____

6. What famous canal helped Chicago become a major commercial center?

   _____

7. What disaster happened in Chicago in 1871?

   _____

8. What is the tallest skyscraper in Chicago?

   _____

9. What new technology did visitors see at the 1893 World's Fair?

   _____

10. What are the major agricultural products of Illinois?

   _____

Activities

Topics for special reports:

Chicago
Hopewell Native Americans
Joliet and Marquette
Skyscrapers

Locate: On the map, put the number for each item in the proper location.

1. Chicago
2. Indiana
3. Iowa
4. Mississippi River
5. Springfield
6. Wisconsin

INDIANA

Indiana means "land of Indians." Native American tribes living in the region included the early mound builders. Several burial mounds remain in the state including the remains of a large village near Newburg. Later Native American tribes included the Kickapoo, Miami, Potawatomi, and Wea.

La Salle and his men visited the region in 1679. The French established early settlements at Vincennes and near the present-day Lafayette and Fort Wayne.

The French surrendered the territory to the British after the French and Indian War in 1763. During the Revolutionary War, American George Rogers Clark defeated the British at the Battle of Vincennes in 1779. Clark and his men later received several thousands of acres reward for their service during the war. They founded Clarksville in 1874.

The territory became a possession of the United States after the Revolutionary War. Indiana became the nineteenth state in 1816.

William Henry Harrison became a national hero after he defeated the Shawnee Indians at the Battle of Tippecanoe. Harrison later became the nation's ninth president. His grandson, Benjamin Harrison, was also a resident of the state. Benjamin Harrison became the nation's twenty-third president. Abraham Lincoln lived in Indiana as a boy. The Lincoln Boyhood National Memorial is a favorite tourist site.

Indiana remained primarily an agricultural state until after the Civil War. Today, it is still a major producer of cattle, hogs, soybeans, corn, and popcorn. It is also a major producer and processor of spearmint and peppermint.

After the Civil War, major industries moved into the state. Automobiles, glass, steel, and other metal production became major industries. Indiana is also a major producer of chemical products.

Indiana has many natural resources including oil, coal, and limestone. Indiana limestone is among the best in the world. It is part of many important buildings including the Empire State Building and several federal buildings in Washington, D.C.

Capital: Indianapolis
Nickname: The Hoosier State
Motto: Crossroads of America
Major Cities: Gary, Fort Wayne, Indianapolis, South Bend
Population: 5,899,000 (est.)
Area: 36,000 square miles, 14th largest
Major Industries: Agriculture, steel, chemicals
Famous Citizens: Benjamin Harrison, Michael Jackson, Cole Porter, David Letterman
Flower: Peony
Tree: Tulip Poplar
Bird: Cardinal

Indiana became the home of several early pioneers of the automobile industry. Elwood Haynes developed an early horseless carriage in 1894.

The Studebaker brothers were in the wagon-building business for several years. They built electric-powered cars in 1902. By 1904, they began building gasoline powered vehicles. The Studebaker factory in South Bend continued to be a major automobile manufacturer until their factory closed in the 1960s. Today, Chrysler, Ford, and General Motors all have plants in Indiana.

Another Indiana connection to the automobile is the Indianapolis 500 race. During the first race in 1911, the top speed was 75 miles per hour. The race continues each year on the Memorial Day weekend. Over half a million fans go to the race each year.

Name: _____ Date: _____

Questions for Consideration

1. What was one of the later Native American tribes in Indiana?

   _____

2. Who were the first Europeans to visit Indiana?

   _____

3. Who defeated the British at the Battle of Vincennes?

   _____

4. When did Indiana become a state?

   _____

5. What grandfather and grandson residents of Indiana both became presidents?

   _____

6. What other president lived in Indiana for a time?

   _____

7. What was Indiana's major economic force before the Civil War?

   _____

8. For what type of building material is Indiana famous?

   _____

9. What type of automobile was made in Indiana from 1902 until 1960?

   _____

10. What famous automobile race is held in Indiana?

   _____

Activities

Topics for special reports:

Battle of Tippecanoe
George Rogers Clark
Benjamin Harrison
La Salle
Limestone
Studebaker

Locate: On the map, put the number for each item in the proper location.

1. Gary
2. Illinois
3. Indianapolis
4. Kentucky
5. Ohio
6. Ohio River

IOWA

Thousands of years ago, a series of glaciers covered most of what is now Iowa. The glaciers leveled mountains and filled valleys. They also left some of the world's richest soil covering the state.

About 1000 B.C., Native Americans known as the Woodland Culture lived in the region. The Mound Builders followed. Over 150 mounds remain in Effigy Mounds National Monument.

Later, members of the Ioway, Illinois, Mesquakie (Fox), Missouri, Omaha, Oto, Ottawa Sauk (Sac), and Sioux tribes lived there. The state was named for the Ioway Native Americans. The word means "beautiful land." Iowa's nickname is the "Hawkeye State." The name honors the Sauk Chief Black Hawk. Today, members of the Mesquakie tribe maintain a reservation near Tama.

During their 1673 trip down the Mississippi River, Louis Joliet and Jacques Marquette were the first whites to see the state. They claimed the territory for France. It was not until 1788 that Julien Dubuque established the first permanent white settlement.

The state came under control of Spain briefly. The French regained control, then sold it to the United States as part of the Louisiana Purchase. Iowa became the twenty-ninth state in 1846.

Several clashes occurred between the white settlers and the Native Americans. The most notable were the Black Hawk War of 1832 and the Spirit Lake Massacre of 1857.

Settlers emigrated to the area because of its rich farm land. Many ethnic groups settled in the state. Danish, Dutch, Swedish, German, Czechoslovakian, Norwegian, Hungarian, and English immigrants all settled in the state. Many Iowa communities continue to hold festivals in honor of their ethnic heritage.

Iowa remained in the Union during the Civil War. It became part of the "underground railroad." This organization (it was not really a railroad) helped slaves from the southern states escape to their freedom.

Herbert Hoover, the thirty-first president, was an Iowan. Hoover, born in West Branch, was the first president born west of the Mississippi River.

Capital: Des Moines
Nickname: The Hawkeye State
Motto: Our Liberties We Prize and Our Rights We Will Maintain
Major Cities: Des Moines, Cedar Rapids, Davenport, Sioux City
Population: 2,862,000 (est.)
Area: 56,290 square miles, 25th largest
Major Industry: Agriculture
Famous Citizens: Herbert Hoover, John Wayne, Grant Wood
Flower: Wild Rose
Tree: Oak
Bird: Eastern Goldfinch

Iowa continues to be a major agricultural state. It is the nation's leading producer of corn and hogs. One-fifth of the nation's corn comes from Iowa. It ties with Illinois as the leading producer of soybeans. Other agricultural products include cattle, sheep, turkeys, oats, rye, barley, and wheat.

The state's largest industry is food processing. Other industries include farm machinery, electrical equipment, and home appliances. Iowa is also a major center for insurance and printing.

Iowa has a varied climate. It has hot, humid summers and cold winters. It is common for the temperature to reach over 100° in summer and several degrees below zero in the winters.

Iowa has been the site of numerous tornadoes and floods. The 1993 and 2008 flooding of the Missouri and Mississippi Rivers devastated the state.

Name: _____ Date: _____

Questions for Consideration

1. What left Iowa with its rich soil?

   _____

2. What does the word *Iowa* (or *Ioway*) mean?

   _____

3. Who does Iowa's nickname honor?

   _____

4. Who were the first white men to see Iowa?

   _____

5. What massacre happened in Iowa?

   _____

6. What organization helped slaves escape to their freedom?

   _____

7. Which president was born in Iowa?

   _____

8. Iowa is the major producer of what type of livestock?

   _____

9. In what crop production does Iowa lead the nation?

   _____

10. What disaster affected Iowa in 1993 and 2008?

   _____

Activities

Topics for special reports:

Corn
Herbert Hoover
Hogs
The Underground Railroad
Mesquakie (or Fox) Native
    Americans

Locate: On the map, put the number for each item in the proper location.

1. Des Moines
2. Cedar Rapids
3. Minnesota
4. Mississippi River
5. Missouri River
6. Nebraska

KANSAS

Tales of gold brought the first Europeans into what is now Kansas. A Spaniard, Francisco Vasquez de Coronado, and his men arrived in 1541.

In 1682, the French became the first to claim the territory. Control over the region went back and forth between the Spanish and French until the French sold it to the United States in the Louisiana Purchase.

Many explorers and settlers traveled through the state. The Lewis and Clark Expedition and Zebulon Pike's Expedition both traveled through Kansas. The Oregon Trail, the Santa Fe Trail, the Chisholm Trail, and the Pony Express route all passed through the state.

Native American tribes to inhabit Kansas included the Arapaho, Cheyenne, Comanche, Kansas, Kiowa, Osage, Pawnee, and Wichita. Early in the state's history, the U.S. government relocated Native American tribes from other states into Kansas. As white settlers continued to arrive, the government relocated the tribes to Oklahoma.

Violence often erupted over the status of slavery in Kansas before the Civil War. In one incident, pro-slavery forces from Missouri raided the town of Lawrence. To get revenge, the abolitionist John Brown and his men murdered five settlers at Pottawatomie Creek. Over 200 people died before the end of the conflict. The state became known as "Bleeding Kansas."

Kansas became the thirty-fourth state in January 1861. It was admitted as a non-slave state. Only months after Kansas became a state, the Civil War began. During the war, William Quantrill and his Confederate raiders burned much of the town and killed over 150 residents of Lawrence. Members of Quantrill's raiders included future outlaw members of the Jesse James and Cole Younger gangs.

Kansas became an important part of the "Old West." Major cattle drives crossed the state. Cowboys moved herds from ranches in Texas to railroads to take them to processing plants. Abilene, Dodge City, and Wichita became noted cowtowns. Dodge City became the most notorious cowtown. Wyatt Earp, Doc Holliday, and Bat Masterson all lived in Dodge City. It is the site of a famous cemetery, Boot Hill.

Kansas is the birthplace of Dwight D. Eisenhower, the thirty-fourth president. Visitors can tour his birthplace in Abilene. The state is also the home of Alf Landon, the 1936, and Robert Dole, the 1996, Republican presidential candidates.

Kansas is the middle of the contiguous (borders touching each other) United States. Before Alaska and Hawaii became states, the geographic middle of the country was near Osborne.

One of Kansas' nicknames is "the Bread Basket of America." The name came from the fact that Kansas is the nation's leading producer of wheat. Other major agricultural products include cattle, corn, and sorghum. The state suffered from the great "Dust Bowl" of the 1930s. A severe drought, lasting about 11 years, ruined most of the crops.

Major industries in Kansas include transportation equipment, food processing, printing, and chemicals.

Capital: Topeka
Nickname: Sunflower State
Motto: To the Stars Through Difficulty
Major Cities: Topeka, Wichita
Population: 2,639,000 (est.)
Area: 82,000 square miles, 14th largest
Major Industries: Agriculture, food products, transportation equipment
Famous Citizens: Emmett Kelly, Carry Nation, Alf Landon
Flower: Sunflower
Tree: Cottonwood
Bird: Western Meadowlark

Name: _____ Date: _____

Questions for Consideration

1. Who were the first Europeans to visit Kansas?

   _____

2. Which country first claimed the region?

   _____

3. What famous mail route went through Kansas?

   _____

4. What nickname did Kansas get because of the violence before the Civil War?

   _____

5. When did Kansas become a state?

   _____

6. What city became the most notorious cowtown?

   _____

7. Which president was born in Kansas?

   _____

8. What two unsuccessful presidential candidates came from Kansas?

   _____

9. What Kansas nickname comes from its production of wheat?

   _____

10. What disaster struck Kansas in the 1930s?

   _____

Activities

Topics for special reports:

Cattle Drives
Chisholm Trail
Wheat
Dwight D. Eisenhower
Francisco Vasquez de
   Coronado

Locate: On the map, put the number for each item in the proper location.

1. Colorado
2. Missouri
3. Nebraska
4. Oklahoma
5. Topeka
6. Wichita
7. Dodge City

KENTUCKY

Kentucky's nickname is "The Bluegrass State." The grass is not really blue. However, when it blooms in late May, the blossoms have a bluish tint.

Nomadic hunters were the first inhabitants of what is now Kentucky. Later, tribes known as Woodlands, then Mound Builders, moved into the region. The Shawnee and Cherokee were the major tribes using the region as hunting grounds at the time of the whites' arrival.

The Appalachian Mountains hindered the early movement of white settlers into Kentucky. A British surveying team discovered the Cumberland Gap in 1750. The Cumberland Gap became the major passage route for settlers traveling from the East.

James Harrod established the first permanent white settlement in the state, Harrodsburg, in 1774. The following year, Daniel Boone led one of the early groups through the Cumberland Gap. They created the settlement of Boonsborough.

The state of Virginia controlled Kentucky at the time of the Revolutionary War. For a while, Kentucky had representatives in the Virginia House of Burgesses. After the War, the number of settlers increased dramatically. The settlers soon demanded independence from Virginia. Kentucky became the fifteenth state in 1792.

Stephen Foster, one of the nation's greatest composers, visited Bardstown in 1852. Many believe that while there, he wrote his most famous song, "My Old Kentucky Home."

Kentucky was a border state during the Civil War. Many plantation owners in the southern part of the state had slaves and wanted to join the Confederacy. Others, such as Henry Clay, wished to abolish slavery and remain in the Union. Kentucky did remain in the Union. However, many of its citizens fought for the Confederacy.

Kentucky was the birthplace of the leaders of both sides of the conflict. The birthplaces of Abraham Lincoln, President of the Union, and Jefferson Davis, President of the Confederacy, are only about 100 miles apart.

The U.S. government established Fort Knox as a military base in 1917. It built the repository to hold much of the nation's gold supply there in 1937. The heavily guarded vault contains billions of dollars worth of gold.

By the end of the nineteenth century, major products of the state included tobacco and coal. Coal was the leading industry for many years. The closing of several coal mines caused great poverty in the rural regions of the state. Modern strip mining techniques continue to cause controversy about the harm to the environment. The tobacco industry also continues to cause controversy.

Kentucky is the center of horse breeding in the nation. The famous Kentucky Derby race began in 1875.

One of Kentucky's important natural wonders is Mammoth Cave. The cave has over 300 miles of pathways.

Capital: Frankfort
Nickname: Bluegrass State
Motto: United We Stand, Divided We Fall
Major Cities: Frankfort, Louisville, Lexington
Population: 3,936,000 (est.)
Area: 40,000 square miles, 37th largest
Major Industries: Agriculture, horses
Famous Citizens: Abraham Lincoln, Jefferson Davis, Muhammad Ali
Flower: Goldenrod
Tree: Kentucky Coffee Tree
Bird: Kentucky Cardinal

Name: _____ Date: _____

Questions for Consideration

1. What is Kentucky's nickname?

   _____

2. What two Native American tribes lived in Kentucky when the first whites arrived?

   _____

3. What became a famous passageway through the Appalachian Mountains?

   _____

4. What famous pioneer led a group into Kentucky?

   _____

5. When did Kentucky become a state?

   _____

6. What noted composer wrote "My Old Kentucky Home"?

   _____

7. What two presidents were born in Kentucky?

   _____

8. What gold repository is in Kentucky?

   _____

9. What famous horse race began in 1875?

   _____

10. What Kentucky cave has over 300 miles of pathways?

   _____

Activities

Topics for special reports:

Daniel Boone
Caves
Henry Clay
Jefferson Davis
Stephen Foster
Fort Knox

Locate: On the map, put the number for each item in the proper location.

1. Cumberland Gap
2. Frankfort
3. Lexington
4. Louisville
5. Ohio River
6. Tennessee

LOUISIANA

The first European to see Louisiana was the Spaniard de Pineda in 1519. In 1541 Hernando de Soto claimed the Mississippi River Valley for Spain.

Later, in 1682, the French entered the region and La Salle claimed the region. La Salle named the territory "Louisiana" in honor of his king, Louis XIV.

French settlers established several settlements in the territory, including New Orleans. The French lost control of Louisiana to the Spanish for almost 40 years. After regaining control, the French sold the region as part of the Louisiana Purchase in 1803. Louisiana became the eighteenth state in 1812.

New Orleans continues to have a strong French influence. The oldest part of the city is still called the French Quarter. Each year, New Orleans is the site of Mardi Gras. The citizens first celebrated this French custom with a parade in 1857. Each year the celebration lasts for several weeks. It ends on the day before Lent.

Early in its history, Louisiana became a melting pot. Arcadians joined Native Americans and French settlers in 1755. The Arcadians were French-Canadians forced out of their homes in Nova Scotia by the British. Descendants of the Arcadians are known as Cajuns.

Many African-Americans living in the region are descendants of slaves brought into the state. Descendants of French and Spanish colonists became known as Creoles. German and Swiss farmers settled beginning in 1718. By the late 1800s, Irish and Italian settlers also arrived.

The Battle of New Orleans was the final battle of the War of 1812. Andrew Jackson, later the nation's seventh president, defeated the British at the famous battle. The battle occurred fifteen days after the official end of the war. Since news traveled so slowly, the generals did not know the war was over.

Louisiana left the Union during the Civil War. At first it declared itself an independent nation, then it later joined the Confederacy. Louisiana rejoined the Union in 1868.

Louisiana has had eleven different constitutions, more than any other state. The state is divided into "parishes" rather than counties.

Capital: Baton Rouge
Nickname: The Pelican State
Motto: Union, Justice, and Confidence
Major Cities: Baton Rouge, New Orleans, Shreveport
Population: 4,369,000 (est.)
Area: 48,000 square miles, 31st largest
Major Industries: Agriculture, oil, chemicals
Famous Citizens: Huey Long, Louis Armstrong
Flower: Magnolia
Tree: Bald Cypress
Bird: Eastern Brown Pelican

Much of Louisiana is low marsh and bayou land. The average altitude of the state is only 100 feet above sea level. New Orleans is actually eight feet below sea level. In 2005, this proved deadly as much of New Orleans flooded when levees failed during hurricane Katrina.

One of Louisiana's most noted citizens, Huey Long, became governor in 1928. Long brought several social reforms and building projects into the state.

Cotton and sugar became major crops during the early eighteenth century. Later, soybeans and rice became of major importance. The discovery of oil in 1901, and later natural gas, added significantly to the state's economy. Much of the oil and natural gas comes from off-shore wells in the Gulf of Mexico. Today, chemical manufacturing is the state's major industry. Louisiana is the nation's leading producer of salt and the second leading state in the production of sulfur.

Name: _____ Date: _____

Questions for Consideration

1. Who claimed the Mississippi River Valley for Spain?

   _____

2. For whom was Louisiana named?

   _____

3. What is the name of the oldest part of New Orleans?

   _____

4. By what name are descendants of the Arcadian settlers known?

   _____

5. By what name are descendants of the French and Spanish settlers known?

   _____

6. What leader won the Battle of New Orleans?

   _____

7. What is the average altitude of Louisiana?

   _____

8. Which hurricane caused deadly floods in New Orleans in 2005?

   _____

9. Who was Louisiana's most famous governor?

   _____

10. What was discovered in Louisiana in 1901?

   _____

Activities

Topics for special reports:

War of 1812
Huey Long
Mardi Gras
New Orleans
Sugar
Dixieland Jazz

Locate: On the map, put the number for each item in the proper location.

1. Baton Rouge
2. Gulf of Mexico
3. Mississippi River
4. New Orleans
5. Shreveport
6. Texas

MAINE

Maine is in the extreme northeastern part of the nation. It borders the Canadian provinces of Quebec and New Brunswick on its north and west sides. Its southern border is with New Hampshire. It is the only state to share a border with just one other state. The eastern side of the state is on the Atlantic Ocean. Offshore Maine contains about 1,100 coastal islands.

Maine's nickname is the "Pine Tree State." Today, forests still cover over 80 percent of its land. The first sawmill opened in 1623.

At one time, the English government ordered that all pine trees over two feet in diameter be reserved for building its ships. Soon after the Revolutionary War, timber and ship building became the state's major industries.

The Algonquin Native Americans populated the state at the time of the arrival of the early European settlers. The Algonquins consisted of people of several tribes using similar customs and language. Many Algonquins died of smallpox brought to America by the white settlers.

Maine's first European visitor may have been the Viking Leif Ericson about 1000 B.C. English explorer John Cabot claimed the region for England about five centuries later. Early French explorers also claimed the territory.

Both the French and English attempted settlements in the early 1600s. The English made the first permanent settlement in 1622. Settlers from the Plymouth, Massachusetts, colony set up a fur trading post at about the same time. French and Indian attacks on British settlements led to the French and Indian Wars.

The Massachusetts Bay Colony annexed the region in 1652. The region remained under British control throughout the Revolutionary War. The first naval battle of the Revolution occurred near Machias. The territory remained under the control of Massachusetts until 1819.

In 1820, Maine became the twenty-third state. Maine was part of the Missouri Compromise. Prior to the Civil War, the national government attempted to keep a balance of the number of slave and non-slave states. To maintain the balance, Maine became a free state at the same time as Missouri joined the Union as a slave state.

The Aroostock War over the Canada-Maine border began in 1839, but no one died in the war. The border finally became established by a treaty in 1842.

Paper manufacturing began after the Civil War, and today, it is Maine's largest industry. The state's forests help supply wood pulp used in paper manufacturing. The second largest industry is lumber.

Other industries developed in the last half of the nineteenth century include textiles and shoemaking.

The fishing industry continues as an important industry. Fishing in its streams as well as along the Atlantic Ocean coast provides a variety of food sources. Maine's most famous seafood is lobster.

Capital: Augusta
Nickname: Pine Tree State
Motto: I Direct
Major Cities: Augusta, Portland, Bangor
Population: 1,244,000 (est.)
Area: 33,000 square miles, 38th largest
Major Industries: Paper and wood products, fishing
Famous Citizens: Stephen King, Edmund Muskie, Henry Wads-worth Longfellow
Flower: White Pine Cone and Tassel
Tree: Eastern White Pine
Bird: Chickadee

Name: _____ Date: _____

Questions for Consideration

1. How many islands are off the coast of Maine?

   _____

2. How much of Maine is covered by forests?

   _____

3. For what purpose did the English government reserve larger pine trees?

   _____

4. What Native Americans lived in Maine at the time of the whites' arrival?

   _____

5. What Viking may have visited Maine?

   _____

6. What Revolutionary War event occurred at Machias?

   _____

7. What state joined the Union at the same time as Maine?

   _____

8. When did the Maine-Canada border become finally established?

   _____

9. What is Maine's largest industry today?

   _____

10. What is Maine's most famous seafood?

   _____

Activities

Topics for special reports:

Algonquins
Leif Ericson
Lobster
Paper
Pine Trees
Missouri Compromise

Locate: On the map, put the number for each item in the proper location.

1. Augusta
2. Atlantic Ocean
3. New Brunswick
4. New Hampshire
5. Portland
6. Quebec (province)

MARYLAND

The Mound Builders were the earliest inhabitants of what is now Maryland. The tribes of the Algonquin and Iroquois nations lived in the region during the arrival of the first whites.

In 1524, the Spanish explorer Giovanni da Verrazano and his men were the first Europeans to visit the region.

Other Spanish explorers sailed into the Chesapeake Bay two years later. The English, under the leadership of Captain John Smith, explored the region in 1608. The first trading post opened in 1631.

King Charles I of England granted land to Lord Baltimore to establish a permanent colony in the New World. Baltimore named the land "Maryland" in honor of the King's wife Queen Henrietta Maria.

Lord Baltimore's son and a group of settlers established the first permanent settlement on Kent Island in 1634. The boundaries between Maryland, Delaware, and Pennsylvania became established in 1767 with a survey of land that established the Mason-Dixon line.

Maryland joined the other colonies in the Revolutionary War. It was the first colony to establish a state constitution. Annapolis was the site of the signing of the treaty ending the Revolutionary War. Annapolis became the nation's capital from November 1783 until August 1784.

Maryland became the seventh state in 1788. In 1791, the citizens of the state gave land to establish the permanent nation's capital, Washington, D.C.

The British troops burned Washington, D.C., during the War of 1812. They then marched to Baltimore. They attacked Fort McHenry near the city. Francis Scott Key saw the battle and later wrote a poem. The poem became the words of the national anthem, "The Star-Spangled Banner."

Maryland was a divided state prior to the Civil War. Southern planters owned slaves and wanted to join the Confederacy. Northern farmers wanted to remain in the Union. The state remained in the Union. However, many of its men fought in the Confederacy. One of the bloodiest battles of the war, Antietam, occurred in the state.

Capital: Annapolis
Nicknames: Free State, Old Line State
Motto: Manly Deeds, Womanly Words
Major Cities: Annapolis, Baltimore
Population: 5,135,000 (est.)
Area: 10,000 square miles, 41st largest
Major Industry: Electronic equipment
Famous Citizens: Samuel Chase, Eubie Blake, Edgar Allan Poe
Flower: Black-eyed Susan
Tree: White Oak
Bird: Baltimore Oriole

Farming and fishing became major industries in the state's early history. Tobacco, wheat, oysters, crabs, and clams became important parts of the economy. Today, Maryland is still famous for its seafood.

Manufacturing became important after the Civil War. The state became a center for shipbuilding, steel, and textiles. The area's major natural resources include coal, stone, clay, sand, and gravel.

Since it borders Washington, D.C., many federal agencies are in Maryland. It is the home of the National Institute of Health, the Bureau of Standards, the Atomic Energy Commission, Goddard Space Flight Center, and many others.

Maryland is also the location of Camp David. Camp David has been a presidential retreat for every president since Franklin D. Roosevelt.

Name: _____ Date: _____

Questions for Consideration

1. What king granted land for the establishment of a settlement in Maryland?

   _____

2. For whom was Maryland named?

   _____

3. Who led the group to found the first settlement?

   _____

4. Where was the treaty signed that ended the Revolutionary War?

   _____

5. For what purpose did Maryland's citizens donate land in 1791?

   _____

6. Who wrote a famous poem about the attack on Fort McHenry?

   _____

7. What major Civil War battle occurred in Maryland?

   _____

8. What were Maryland's early major industries?

   _____

9. Why is Maryland the location of many federal agencies?

   _____

10. What presidential retreat is in Maryland?

   _____

Activities

Topics for special reports:

Annapolis
Antietam
Lord Baltimore
   (father and son)
Camp David
Mason-Dixon Line

Locate: On the map, put the number for each item in the proper location.

1. Annapolis
2. Baltimore
3. Delaware
4. Pennsylvania
5. Virginia
6. Washington, D.C.

MASSACHUSETTS

Algonquin tribes inhabited Massachusetts when the first Europeans arrived in the region. Vikings may have visited the coastline as early as the year 1000. The English explorer John Cabot arrived in 1498. Shortly after his arrival, English, French, Spanish, and Portuguese began fishing in the area.

The most famous early settlers were the Pilgrims. They arrived in Massachusetts in 1620. They established a settlement at Plymouth after a 65-day voyage on the *Mayflower.* The following year, the Pilgrims invited local Native Americans to join them for the first American Thanksgiving celebration. The Native Americans welcomed the settlers and often helped them with gifts of food. They also taught the settlers how to plant native crops. However, conflicts between the two groups arose as more settlers arrived. A series of wars between the Native American tribes and the settlers occurred between 1637 and 1676.

In 1636, Harvard College, later renamed Harvard University, became the first college in the United States.

Disputes began between the colonists and the British government. King Charles II canceled Massachusetts's charter in 1682. The colonists then set up their own government.

Massachusetts was of vital importance during the Revolutionary War. The Boston Tea Party of 1773 was one of the major events to cause the war. The first shots of the war occurred at Lexington in 1775. The patriots won their first battle of the war at Concord. Paul Revere made his famous midnight ride through the streets of Boston.

Today, Boston is the location of many sites associated with the Revolution. They include the Old South Meeting House, Paul Revere's House, and the Old North Church. The USS *Constitution*, a famous ship from the War of 1812 known as "Old Ironsides," is also in Boston Harbor.

In 1788, Massachusetts became the sixth state to join the union.

Massachusetts is the birthplace of four presidents. John Adams and his son John Quincy Adams were natives of Quincy. John Kennedy was born in Brookline. George Bush was from Milton. The Adams' home in Quincy and the Kennedy Library in Boston are popular visitors' sites. President Calvin Coolidge was born in Vermont, but moved to Massachusetts; before becoming president, he was a governor of Massachusetts, and he retired there after his presidency.

James Naismith invented basketball in 1891. He created the game by hanging peach baskets at each end of the YMCA in Springfield.

Massachusetts is the home of many literary figures. Henry David Thoreau, Ralph Waldo Emerson, Nathaniel Hawthorne, the Alcotts, the poetess Emily Dickinson, and Dr. Seuss all lived in the state. Other famous Massachusetts natives include Susan B. Anthony, Samuel Morse, Eli Whitney, and Clara Barton.

Early industries in Massachusetts included fishing, fur trading, lumber, and shipbuilding. The textile industry began in the state at the beginning of the 1800s. Scientists developed the first computer at Massachusetts Institute of Technology in 1928.

Capital: Boston
Nickname: Bay State
Motto: By the Sword We Seek Peace, but Peace Only Under Liberty
Major Cities: Boston, Springfield
Population: 6,147,000 (est.)
Area: 8,000 square miles, 45th largest
Major Industry: Electronic equipment
Famous Citizens: John Adams, John Quincy Adams, John Kennedy, Paul Revere, Susan B. Anthony
Flower: Mayflower
Tree: American Elm
Bird: Chickadee

42

Name: _____ Date: _____

Questions for Consideration

1. What noted English explorer visited Massachusetts in 1498?

   _____

2. Who were the most famous early settlers of Massachusetts?

   _____

3. What was the name of the first college in the United States?

   _____

4. What Massachusetts event helped begin the Revolutionary War?

   _____

5. Who made a famous ride through the streets of Boston?

   _____

6. Who was the last American president to be born in Massachusetts?

   _____

7. What did James Naismith invent?

   _____

8. What famous poetess lived in Massachusetts?

   _____

9. What became the major industry in Massachusetts in the early 1800s?

   _____

10. Scientists developed what famous invention at Massachusetts Institute of Technology?

   _____

Activities

Topics for special reports:

Harvard
Old Ironsides
Pilgrims
Paul Revere
Thanksgiving
Vikings

Locate: On the map, put the number for each item in the proper location.

1. Atlantic Ocean
2. Boston
3. Connecticut
4. New Hampshire
5. Plymouth
6. Vermont

MICHIGAN

Michigan's name comes from the Chippewa Native American word *Michigama*. *Michigama* means "great lake." Michigan has shores on four of the five Great Lakes. Lakes Erie, Huron, Michigan, and Superior all form parts of the state's border.

Michigan is made up of two large peninsulas. The Upper Peninsula (known as the UP) connects to Wisconsin, but not the rest of Michigan. The Lower Peninsula connects the state to Indiana and Ohio. The Mackinac Bridge opened in 1957. Nicknamed "Big Mac," the bridge connects the two peninsulas. Big Mac is five miles long, making it the world's fourth longest suspension bridge.

Early European explorers of the region were French. Etienne Brule explored the Upper Peninsula in 1620. Louis Joliet became the first European to explore the Lower Peninsula in 1669. Father Jacques Marquette established the first permanent settlement by 1668. La Salle and his men built the first French fort in the region in 1679.

In 1763, the British gained control of the region at the end of the French and Indian War. The settlers supported the British government during the Revolutionary War. The territory did not come under U.S. control until 1796. The British regained control of the region briefly during the War of 1812.

Large numbers of settlers entered the region after the opening of the Erie Canal in 1825. The Erie Canal provided cheap and convenient transportation of goods and passengers from the Great Lakes to the eastern states and to the Atlantic Ocean.

Michigan became the twenty-sixth state in 1837.

Early industries in the state included fur trading, agriculture, and minerals. Native Americans mined copper long before the coming of the whites. Iron ore and salt joined copper as major products of the state. At the end of the nineteenth century, the automobile industry began in Michigan. R. E. Olds made a steam powered car in 1886. He established the first automobile factory in the United States in Detroit in 1900. Henry Ford opened his factory, also in Detroit, in 1903. General Motors opened its Detroit factory in 1908. Walter Chrysler opened the Chrysler Corporation in the city in 1925.

Detroit quickly became the world's largest producer of automobiles. It soon had the nickname "Motor City" or "Motown." "Motown" is also the name of a style of popular music that originated in Detroit.

John Harvey Kellogg developed a way to turn wheat into precooked flakes. He invented the first breakfast cereal. He opened a factory to make wheat flakes in 1895. In 1906, John's younger brother, Keith, introduced corn flakes. Charles W. Post soon introduced his version of cereal, Post Toasties®. Battle Creek soon became the nation's cereal capital.

Gerald R. Ford represented Michigan in the U.S. House of Representatives. He became the vice president when Vice President Spiro Agnew resigned. Ford then became the president when Richard Nixon resigned in 1974.

Capital: Lansing
Nickname: Wolverine State
Motto: If You Seek a Pleasant Peninsula, Look About You
Major Cities: Detroit, Flint, Grand Rapids, Lansing
Population: 9,817,000 (est.)
Area: 58,500 square miles, 23rd largest
Major Industries: Automobiles, agriculture
Famous Citizens: Gerald Ford, Malcolm X, Aretha Franklin
Flower: Apple Blossom
Tree: White Pine
Bird: Robin

Name: _____ Date: _____

Questions for Consideration

1. How many of the Great Lakes touch Michigan?

_____

2. When referring to Michigan, what does "UP" mean?

_____

3. What famous bridge connects the two main parts of Michigan?

_____

4. Who built the first French fort in the region?

_____

5. What canal helped settle Michigan?

_____

6. Who established the first automobile factory in the United States?

_____

7. What is the name of the popular music style that came from Detroit?

_____

8. Who invented the first breakfast cereal?

_____

9. What did Charles W. Post invent?

_____

10. What president was from Michigan?

_____

Activities

Topics for special reports:

Chippewa Native Americans
Henry Ford
Great Lakes
John and Keith Kellogg
Suspension Bridges
Gerald R. Ford

Locate: On the map, put the number for each item in the proper location.

1. Detroit
2. Lake Huron
3. Lake Michigan
4. Lake Superior
5. Lansing
6. Upper Peninsula
7. Lake Erie

MINNESOTA

The first people to live in what is now Minnesota probably came over a land bridge in the Bering Sea. They arrived around 9000 B.C. The Woodland Culture thrived from about 1000 B.C. until 1500. Mound Builders arrived later. Over 10,000 of their mounds still survive in the state. The mounds are in the shape of bears, bison, birds, and snakes.

Native American tribes living in the region when the first Europeans arrived included the Sioux and Ojibwa (or Chippewa). The first Europeans in the region may have been the Vikings. In 1898, a farmer discovered a stone with writing carved into it. The stone, known as the Kensington Rune Stone, told of a visit by the Vikings in 1362. The stone caused controversy. Many historians believe that the stone is a fake.

French explorers entered the region in 1660. French and British fur traders soon began working there. The French claimed the region and built forts such as Fort St. Charles and Fort Antoine to protect their interests.

The French ceded the territory to the British and Spanish after the French and Indian War. The United States took control of the land east of the Mississippi River in 1783. The rest of the state came under U.S. control as part of the Louisiana Purchase. Minnesota became the thirty-second state in 1858.

A series of conflicts arose between white settlers and Native American tribes. Over 400 whites died in the Sioux revolt of 1862.

"Land of a Thousand Lakes" is one of Minnesota's many nicknames. The name "Minnesota" comes from Dakota Sioux words meaning "sky-colored water." Minnesota contains over 15,000 lakes in addition to thousands of smaller ponds. It is also the site of the beginning of the Mississippi River. Minnesota received much damage during the 1993 flood of the Mississippi and other rivers.

Fur trading was the first major industry of the region. As settlers, mainly Scandinavians, arrived, farming, dairy cattle, and lumber became of greater economic importance. The coming of the railroads in the 1860s aided the farmers in getting their produce to markets farther away.

Wheat became the major crop. Several mills were built to grind the wheat into flour. One of Minnesota's many nicknames is the "Bread and Butter State" since it is one of the nations' major producers of flour and dairy products.

Miners discovered iron ore in the 1880s. The mining industry grew rapidly. Minnesota provides much of the nation's iron ore. It is shipped across the Great Lakes to steel-producing cities in Pennsylvania, Ohio, and Indiana. Minnesota also mines large amounts of rock products including granite, limestone, sand, and gravel.

The St. Lawrence Seaway opened in 1959. This allowed large ocean-going ships to travel all of the way from the Atlantic Ocean to Lake Superior. Duluth soon became a major world shipping port.

Capital: St. Paul
Nickname: North Star State, Gopher State
Motto: The Star of the North
Major Cities: Bloomington, Duluth, Minneapolis, St. Paul
Population: 4,725,000 (est.)
Area: 84,400 square miles, 12th largest
Major Industries: Agriculture, mining
Famous Citizens: Warren Burger, Judy Garland, Hubert Humphrey
Flower: Pink and White Lady's Slipper
Tree: Red Pine or Norway Pine
Bird: Common Loon

Name: _____ Date: _____

Questions for Consideration

1. How many Native American mounds survive in Minnesota?

   _____

2. Who may have been the first Europeans to visit Minnesota?

   _____

3. Why did the French build Fort St. Charles?

   _____

4. When did Minnesota become a state?

   _____

5. What do the Dakota Sioux words for Minnesota mean?

   _____

6. Why is Minnesota named the "Bread and Butter State"?

   _____

7. What major industry began in Minnesota in the 1880s?

   _____

8. What allowed ocean-going ships to travel to Minnesota?

   _____

9. How is iron ore shipped to steel-producing cities?

   _____

10. What major disaster occurred in Minnesota in 1993?

    _____

Activities

Topics for special reports:

Iron (iron ore)
Lakes
Mound Builders
St. Lawrence Seaway

Locate: On the map, put the number for each item in the proper location.

1. Canada
2. Duluth
3. Iowa
4. Lake Superior
5. Minneapolis/St. Paul
6. Wisconsin

MISSISSIPPI

Native Americans known as the Temple Mound Builders lived in Mississippi in about 700 A.D. Several of the mounds still exist, including one of the largest, Emerald Mound, near Natchez. Major Native American tribes in the region when Europeans first arrived included the Chickasaw, Choctaw, and Natchez.

Spanish explorer Hernando de Soto was the first European to see Mississippi. He and his men came into the region to find gold. They never found the gold for which they were searching. However, they did discover the Mississippi River in 1541. De Soto returned to the region in 1542 and died there.

The Frenchman La Salle arrived in 1682. He claimed the territory for France. Several French settlers soon moved into the region. In 1699, they built the first fort, Fort Maurepas, and the first permanent white settlement near Ocean Springs.

The French also established Natchez on the Mississippi River in 1817. It began as a trading post for furs. It later became an important cotton shipping port. Natchez was the end of the famous Natchez Trace. This was a 450-mile trail from Nashville, Tennessee, to Natchez. Originally an Indian trail, later many pioneers traveled on the Trace during their migration westward.

The French ceded the land to the British at the end of the French and Indian War. In 1781 the Spanish captured the territory from the British. Six years later, the Spanish ceded the land to the United States. Mississippi became the twentieth state in 1817.

Mississippi was the second state to leave the Union at the beginning of the Civil War. Jefferson Davis served as a senator from Mississippi and U.S. Secretary of State before becoming the President of the Confederacy. Davis's childhood home, Rosemont Plantation, and his last home, Beauvoir, are popular visitors' sites.

Many Civil War battles raged in Mississippi. The most noted was the battle of Vicksburg. The siege of the city lasted for 47 days before General Ulysses S. Grant claimed the city for the Union.

Cotton became the major crop of Mississippi in the early nineteenth century. After the devastation of the Civil War and the damage caused by the boll weevil, Mississippi became one of the poorest states in the nation.

Capital: Jackson
Nickname: The Magnolia State
Motto: By Valor and Arms
Major Cities: Biloxi, Jackson, Meridian, Hattiesburg
Population: 2,752,000 (est.)
Area: 47,700 square miles, 32nd largest
Major Industry: Textiles
Famous Citizens: William Faulkner, Elvis Presley, John Grisham
Flower: Magnolia
Tree: Magnolia
Bird: Mockingbird

The civil rights movement was hotly debated in Mississippi. The state enacted several laws enforcing segregation and limiting rights of African-Americans. James Meredith became the first African-American to attend the University of Mississippi. His admittance to the school set off a series of violent protests. In 1963, Medgar Evers, an official of the NAACP, was murdered in front of his home in Jackson.

Mississippi is the birthplace of several musicians. Elvis Presley, B.B. King, Charlie Pride, Jimmie Rodgers, and Tammy Wynette are all natives of Mississippi. Writers born in Mississippi include William Faulkner and Tennessee Williams.

Mississippi and other Gulf Coast states suffered extensive damage from hurricane Katrina in 2005.

Name: _____ Date: _____

Questions for Consideration

1. Who was the first European explorer to see Mississippi?

   _____

2. Who claimed the territory for France?

   _____

3. Why was Natchez established?

   _____

4. When did the United States gain control of Mississippi?

   _____

5. What is Beauvoir?

   _____

6. What was the most important battle of the Civil War to occur in Mississippi?

   _____

7. What was the most important crop in Mississippi in the nineteenth century?

   _____

8. Who was the first African-American to attend the University of Mississippi?

   _____

9. What civil rights leader was murdered in front of his home in Jackson?

   _____

10. What famous rock and roll singer was born in Mississippi?

    _____

Activities

Topics for special reports:

Civil Rights Movement
Plantations
Natchez (Natchez Trace)

Locate: On the map, put the number for each item in the proper location.

1. Alabama
2. Jackson
3. Gulf of Mexico
4. Louisiana
5. Mississippi River
6. Natchez

MISSOURI

The earliest inhabitants of Missouri were the Bluff Shelter People. They lived in shallow caves over 4,000 years ago. The Hopewell Culture moved into the region about 2,000 years ago. They were Mound Builders. Several of their burial mounds remain in the state.

By the time of the arrival of the first Europeans, the major groups of Native Americans were the Missouri, Iowa, Sauk, Fox, and Osage. The word *Missouri* was originally the name of a Native American tribe. It meant "people of the long canoes." The tribe members hollowed out large logs to use as canoes. The state and the river were named after the Missouri tribe.

The Mississippi River forms the state's eastern border. The Missouri River forms the upper western border, and then cuts through the middle of the state to join the Mississippi.

The French were the first to explore and claim the territory. Jacques Marquette and Louis Joliet visited Missouri on their 1673 trip down the Mississippi River. La Salle claimed the territory for France in 1682. In 1735 the first permanent white settlement began at Ste. Genevieve. Control over the territory went to Spain and then back to the French until the United States bought the land as part of the Louisiana Purchase.

Pierre Laclede started a trading post where the Mississippi and Missouri Rivers join. He named the settlement near his post St. Louis, after a French king. St. Louis became one of the major places where settlers moving west began their journey; it became known as the "Gateway to the West." Today, a 630-foot stainless steel arch called the Jefferson National Expansion Memorial commemorates the westward movement.

Settlers continued to pour into the state from the East. Daniel Boone settled in Missouri in 1799. Both the Sante Fe Trail and the Oregon Trail began at Independence.

Missouri became the twenty-fourth state in 1821. It was a slave state. To maintain a balance of free and slave states, Maine became a free state at the same time.

The Pony Express began in 1860 in St. Joseph. Riders delivered mail from St. Joseph to San Francisco in just ten days. Buffalo Bill Cody and Wild Bill Hickok both rode for the Pony Express. The service lasted for just over one year. When workers completed the transcontinental telegraph line, the Pony Express became obsolete.

Even though it was a slave state, Missouri remained in the Union. Several skirmishes happened in the state during the Civil War. After the war, Jesse James and his gang began their criminal careers.

One of the state's most famous citizens was Mark Twain. Twain used his experiences growing up in Missouri as the basis of his books. Visitors can still see his birthplace in Florida, Missouri, and his boyhood home in Hannibal. Lamar was the birthplace of Harry S Truman who grew up in Independence. He was a senator before becoming the vice president and president of the United States. Walt Disney is another noted Missourian. He had an animation studio in Kansas City before moving to California.

Capital: Jefferson City
Nickname: The Show-Me State
Motto: The Welfare of the People Shall be the Supreme Law
Major Cities: St. Louis, Kansas City, Springfield, Jefferson City
Population: 5,439,000 (est.)
Area: 69,700 square miles, 19th largest
Major Industry: Agriculture, manufacturing
Famous Citizens: Jesse James, Harry Truman, George W. Carver
Flower: Hawthorn
Tree: Dogwood
Bird: Bluebird

Name: _____ Date: _____

Questions for Consideration

1. What did the Native American word *Missouri* mean?

   _____

2. For whom was St. Louis named?

   _____

3. What monument commemorates the westward movement?

   _____

4. What famous pioneer settled in Missouri in 1799?

   _____

5. What state entered the Union at the same time as Missouri?

   _____

6. What mail service began in St. Joseph in 1860?

   _____

7. Who is Missouri's most infamous criminal?

   _____

8. What famous writer grew up in Missouri?

   _____

9. What president came from Missouri?

   _____

10. Who once had an animation studio in Kansas City?

    _____

Activities

Topics for special reports:

Canoes
Mark Twain
Jesse James
The Pony Express
Harry S Truman

Locate: On the map, put the number for each item in the proper location.

1. Iowa
2. Jefferson City
3. Kansas City
4. St. Louis
5. Mississippi River
6. Missouri River

MONTANA

Montana's nickname is the "Treasure State." This refers to the state's deposits of valuable minerals. These include gold, copper, silver, zinc, oil, and coal.

Grassland great plains cover the eastern two-thirds of the state. The Rocky Mountains cover the western third of the land. *Montana* is a Spanish word meaning "mountain."

Numerous Native American tribes lived and hunted in the region. Members of the Arapaho, Assiniboin, Atsina, Bannock, Blackfoot, Cheyenne, Crow, Kalispel, Salish, and Shoshone lived in the state. The Nez Perce, Sioux, and Mandan hunted in the region. Today, members of 12 tribes live in Montana. The state contains seven reservations. Two famous battles between the U.S. government and Native American tribes occurred in Montana. On June 25, 1876, 15,000 Sioux and Cheyenne warriors under Chief Crazy Horse defeated 700 soldiers under Lieutenant Colonel George Custer. Custer and 265 of his men were killed. The battle at the Little Big Horn River became known as "Custer's Last Stand." Soldiers and settlers defeated Nez Perce warriors under Chief Joseph on October 5, 1877. At the time of his defeat, Chief Joseph said, "The little children are freezing to death. My heart is sick and sad. From where the sun now stands, I will fight no more forever."

Eastern Montana was part of the Louisiana Purchase. Great Britain ceded the remainder of the state to the United States under the 1846 Oregon Treaty.

French fur traders came through the region in 1743. Members of the Lewis and Clark Expedition of 1805 crossed through Montana. They also visited the area on their 1806 return trip. The expedition identified many plants and animals during the trip. They were the first Europeans to note the state bird (western meadowlark), flower (bitterroot), fish (cutthroat trout), grass (bluebunch wheatgrass), and tree (Ponderosa pine). After the Lewis and Clark Expedition, fur traders and later miners settled in the region. Fort Benton was the first permanent settlement. Established in 1847, it was an outpost of the American Fur Company.

Prospectors discovered gold near Drummond in 1858 and at Grasshopper Creek in 1862. Montana's cattle industry began in 1860. Ranchers drove longhorns from Texas into the region.

Montana became part of the Idaho Territory in 1863. President Lincoln established the Montana Territory the following year. Montana became the forty-first state in 1889.

Montana sent the first woman, Jeanette Rankin, to the U.S. House of Representatives in 1916.

Tourism is an important part of Montana's economy. The northern part of Yellowstone National Park is in Montana. Yellowstone was the first national park ever established. Montana also contains Glacier National Park, Little Bighorn National Monument, The Bighorn Canyon National Recreation Area, and several national forests and monuments.

Tourism, mining, and cattle remain among Montana's major industries. The state is also an important producer of sheep, wheat, lumber, and wood products.

Capital: Helena
Nickname: The Treasure State
Motto: Gold and Silver
Major Cities: Billings, Helena, Great Falls
Population: 880,000 (est.)
Area: 147,000 square miles, 4th largest
Major Industries: Agriculture, mining
Famous Citizens: Gary Cooper, Chet Huntley, Myrna Loy
Flower: Bitterroot
Tree: Ponderosa Pine
Bird: Western Meadowlark

Name: _____ Date: _____

Questions for Consideration

1. What is Montana's nickname?

   _____

2. What does the Spanish word *montana* mean?

   _____

3. How many Native American reservations does Montana have?

   _____

4. Who came into the region in 1743?

   _____

5. What famous expedition explored Montana in 1805 and 1806?

   _____

6. When did Montana's cattle industry begin?

   _____

7. What battle took place in Montana in 1876?

   _____

8. Who was the famous chief of the Nez Perce?

   _____

9. Who was the first woman to serve in the U.S. House of Representatives?

   _____

10. What was the first national park to be established?

   _____

Activities

Topics for special reports:

Chief Joseph
Lt. Col. George Custer
Chief Crazy Horse
Sheep

Locate: On the map, put the number for each item in the proper location.

1. Billings
2. Canada
3. Helena
4. Idaho
5. North Dakota
6. Wyoming

NEBRASKA

Nebraska is one of the states of the Great Plains region. Settlement of the area was difficult. Few trees grew in the region to provide lumber and shade. The sod was thick and difficult to make into farms. Drought and wind storms added to the difficulties of living in the territory. The land soon earned the nickname "the Great American Desert."

Native Americans inhabited or hunted in the region for at least 12,000 years. Members of the Arapaho, Cheyenne, Omaha, Oto, Pawnee, Ponca, and Sioux tribes inhabited the land at the time of the arrival of the first Europeans.

Spanish soldiers under the leadership of Pedro de Villasur were the first Europeans to visit the region. La Salle claimed the territory for France in 1682. Spanish, French, and Mexican governments all fought to control the land. The United States bought the territory as part of the Louisiana Purchase.

The Lewis and Clark Expedition explored the region in 1804. In 1819, the government built Ft. Atkinson. It was the first military post established west of the Missouri River.

Many settlers passed through Nebraska on their way westward. About 300,000 people crossed the state between 1840 and 1860. The Oregon Trail, the Mormon Trail, and the California Trail all crossed Nebraska. Few remained in the state because of the difficulty of living on the prairie.

Settlers began to remain in the region by the 1860s. The Homestead Act of 1862 gave land to those who would settle and develop the land. Homesteaders received 160 acres of land for a small fee. At about the same time, the railroads moved into the region. This allowed for easy transportation of people into the area as well as farm products to eastern markets. Nebraska became the thirty-seventh state in 1867.

Nebraska has a unique form of government. It is the only state to have a unicameral legislature. It has only one legislative body instead of two (a house of representatives and a senate) as in all of the other states.

Corn became the major crop of early farmers. It is still the state's largest crop. Nebraska's nickname is "the Cornhusker State." Cattle and hogs soon became major products of the region.

Capital: Lincoln
Nickname: The Cornhusker State
Motto: Equality Before the Law
Major Cities: Lincoln, Omaha
Population: 1,663,000 (est.)
Area: 77,300 square miles, 15th largest
Major Industry: Agriculture
Famous Citizens: Henry Fonda, Father Flanagan, Willa Cather, Johnny Carson
Flower: Goldenrod
Tree: Cottonwood
Bird: Western Meadowlark

Today, over half of the state's population works in agriculture-related occupations.

Drillers discovered oil in Nebraska in 1939. The state is now a producer of both oil and natural gas.

One of Nebraska's most famous citizens was William Jennings Bryan. Bryan was born in Illinois and then moved to Nebraska in 1887. He represented the state in Congress before running for president three times. Bryan was the unsuccessful candidate in 1896, 1900, and 1908.

Another important Nebraskan was Father Edward Flanagan. He established Boys Town in 1917. Flanagan's motto was, "There is no such thing as a bad boy." Thousands of boys, and in later years girls, lived at Boys Town.

Name: _____ Date: _____

Questions for Consideration

1. What nickname did Nebraska earn because of its climate?

   _____

2. Who claimed the region for France?

   _____

3. Who explored the region in 1804?

   _____

4. What was the first fort built in Nebraska?

   _____

5. What Act helped settlers locate in Nebraska?

   _____

6. What is the name of the type of legislature used by Nebraska?

   _____

7. What is Nebraska's largest agricultural crop?

   _____

8. What are Nebraska's other major agricultural products?

   _____

9. Who lived in Nebraska and ran for president three times?

   _____

10. Who founded Boys Town?

   _____

Activities

Topics for special reports:

Boys Town
The Great Plains
The Homestead Act
The Mormon Trail
William Jennings Bryan

Locate: On the map, put the number for each item in the proper location.

1. Iowa
2. Kansas
3. Lincoln
4. Omaha
5. Missouri River
6. South Dakota

NEVADA

Nevada is a Spanish word for "snow-covered." The name came from the snow-topped Sierra Nevada mountain range. These mountains are on the western border of the state. The mountains are tall enough that they block clouds from the West. Without the rain from these clouds, much of Nevada remains a desert.

The first Europeans to visit the region did not arrive until 1775. The Spanish priest Father Francisco Garcés was the first white to explore the southern part of the state. Others soon explored the state including British and American trappers. Mexico controlled the region until after the Mexican War. The first official expeditions were those of Capt. John C. Frémont between 1843 and 1845. The U.S. government gained control of the territory as part of the 1848 Treaty of Guadelupe Hidalgo.

Mormons established the first permanent white settlement, Mormon Station (now Genoa), in 1850. Seven years later, they moved from Nevada to resettle in Utah. Nevada was originally part of the Utah territory. It became the Nevada territory in 1861. Nevada became the thirty-sixth state in 1864. Abraham Lincoln's supporters rushed through the statehood process to get two more votes to pass the thirteenth amendment to the Constitution, which abolished slavery.

A famous gold and silver discovery, the Comstock Lode, occurred in 1859. The Comstock was the richest discovery in the nation's history. The gold and silver rush brought many settlers into the state. Nevada's nickname is "the Silver State." Nevada's economy suffered when the Comstock Lode was mined out. Many towns such as Virginia City and several sites near Ely became ghost towns after the mines failed. Interest in mining revived after the discovery of ore at Tonopah and Goldfield in 1900.

In the early twentieth century, irrigation of mountain valleys began. Raising sheep and some crops began. Today, cattle, sheep, and hog production account for over half of the state's agricultural income.

Capital: Carson City
Nickname: The Silver State
Motto: All for Our Country
Major Cities: Carson City, Las Vegas, Reno
Population: 1,747,000 (est.)
Area: 110,500 square miles, 7th largest
Major Industries: Gambling, mining, concrete
Famous Citizens: Walter Van Tilburgh Clark, Pat McCarran, Andre Agassi, Sarah Winnemucca Hopkins
Flower: Sagebrush
Trees: Single-leaf Piñon and Bristlecone Pine
Bird: Mountain Bluebird

Workers completed construction on Boulder Dam (now Hoover Dam) in 1935. It was the world's highest dam at the time of its construction. In addition to providing flood control, the dam generates large amounts of electrical power.

Nevada legalized gambling in 1931. Gambling soon became the state's largest industry. The gambling industry contributed to the fact that from 1960 to 1980 Nevada was the nation's fastest-growing state. Las Vegas and Reno became leading gambling and entertainment centers. In recent years, Las Vegas has been the site of many new hotels. The MGM Grand, built in 1993, has 5,000 rooms. It is the largest hotel in the world. Tourism continues to be a major industry. One out of three jobs in Nevada is related to tourism.

Nevada became a testing site for the federal government in 1951. It is the site of the Nellis Air Force Range and the Atomic Energy Commission Nuclear Testing Area.

Name: _____ Date: _____

Questions for Consideration

1. What does the Spanish word *Nevada* mean?

    _____

2. What mountains are on the western border of Nevada?

    _____

3. Who was the first European to explore what is now Nevada?

    _____

4. Who led the first official expeditions into the region?

    _____

5. What treaty gave control of the region to the United States?

    _____

6. What was the name of the gold and silver discovery of 1859?

    _____

7. What is Nevada's nickname?

    _____

8. What is the current name of Boulder Dam?

    _____

9. What large hotel opened in Las Vegas in 1993?

    _____

10. What did Nevada become for the federal government in 1951?

    _____

Activities

Topics for special reports:

Boulder Dam
John C. Frémont
Mexican-American War
Sierra Nevada Mountains
Virginia City (or ghost towns)

Locate: On the map, put the number for each item in the proper location.

1. California
2. Carson City
3. Colorado River
4. Las Vegas
5. Reno
6. Utah

NEW HAMPSHIRE

New Hampshire's nickname is "the Granite State." The name came from the red and gray granite of the White Mountain Range. The White Mountain Range runs through New Hampshire. It is the northern part of the Appalachian Mountains. Mt. Washington, which rises 6,288 feet above sea level, is the highest point in the state. Mt. Washington holds the record for the highest wind ever recorded. In 1934, winds reached 231 miles per hour. A rock formation in the White Mountains that looks like an old man's face became the state's official emblem in 1945.

The first known European to visit New Hampshire was an English captain, Martin Pring. He and his men visited the coast in 1603. Early English and French explorers encountered members of the Algonquin tribes. As Europeans continued to settle the region, the Native American tribes moved out of the region.

The English government granted land in the region to John Mason. Mason was from Hampshire County, England. He named the new land "New Hampshire." In 1623, English settlers, under the leadership of David Tomson, established the first permanent settlement near what is now Portsmouth.

New Hampshire became an important shipbuilding location despite the fact that it had only eighteen miles of coastline. By the mid 1700s, Portsmouth became a major port. A New Hampshire company built John Paul Jones's famous ship *Bonhomme Richard*.

Massachusetts governed the territory at various times. New Hampshire became a separate province in 1692. New Hampshire was the first state to create an independent government. It adopted its own constitution in January 1776. It was one of the original thirteen colonies and became the ninth state to ratify the Constitution in 1788.

New Hampshire native Franklin Pierce became the fourteenth President of the United States in 1852. Pierce was born at Hillsboro and lived in Concord. Today, visitors can see his family's homestead at Hillsboro.

The textile industry began in the state at the beginning of the nineteenth century. The industry reached its peak at the beginning of the twentieth century. As the importance of the textile industry declined, timber and paper manufacturing became the state's major industries.

In 1905, President Theodore Roosevelt invited negotiators to peace talks at Portsmouth. The settlement ended with the signing of the Treaty of Portsmouth, which ended the Russo-Japanese War.

New Hampshire again became the location of international attention when it became the location of the 1944 International Monetary Conference. The delegates to the conference helped plan the World Bank and the International Monetary Fund.

New Hampshire takes on increased political importance in each presidential election year. It is the site of the first presidential primary election. This primary often indicates who will become the major candidates for each political party.

Capital: Concord
Nickname: The Granite State
Motto: Live Free or Die
Major Cities: Concord, Manchester
Population: 1,185,000 (est.)
Area: 9,200 square miles, 44th largest
Major Industries: Timber, paper
Famous Citizens: Franklin Pierce, Christa McAuliffe, Daniel Webster, Mary Baker Eddy, Daniel Chester French, Horace Greeley
Flower: Purple Lilac
Tree: White Birch
Bird: Purple Finch

Name: _____ Date: _____

Questions for Consideration

1. What mountain range runs through New Hampshire?

   _____

2. What is the highest point in New Hampshire?

   _____

3. What was the record wind recorded in New Hampshire?

   _____

4. What Native American tribe lived in New Hampshire when the first whites arrived?

   _____

5. What was the name of John Paul Jones's ship?

   _____

6. Which U.S. president was born in New Hampshire?

   _____

7. What was New Hampshire's major industry in the nineteenth century?

   _____

8. What treaty ended the Russo-Japanese War?

   _____

9. What international conference occurred in New Hampshire in 1944?

   _____

10. What important political event occurs in New Hampshire each presidential election year?

   _____

Activities

Topics for special reports:

Textiles
Appalachian Mountains
John Paul Jones
Granite
Franklin Pierce

Locate: On the map, put the number for each item in the proper location.

1. Atlantic Ocean
2. Canada
3. Concord
4. Maine
5. Massachusetts
6. Vermont

NEW JERSEY

New Jersey is primarily an industrial state. However, its nickname is "the Garden State." The nickname came from its many fruit orchards and vegetable farms.

The Lenni Lenape were the first people to live in the region. They were members of the Algonquin speaking tribes. Almost all Native American tribes moved west out of the state by 1800.

In 1524 Giovanni da Verrazano and his crew were the first Europeans to see what is now New Jersey. Henry Hudson claimed the region for the Netherlands in 1609. The territory became New Netherlands by 1626. Dutch settlers under the leadership of Peter Stuyvesant arrived in 1655. They established the first permanent town, Bergen, in 1660. The British soon claimed the territory. In 1664, Stuyvesant surrendered control to the British. The British renamed the region "New Jersey" after Jersey, an island in the English Channel.

New Jersey became important during the Revolutionary War. The land was of importance because of its location between New York City and Philadelphia. Soldiers fought several major battles on New Jersey's soil. The Battle of Trenton and the Battle of Monmouth were the most important battles. Two New Jersey cities served briefly as the nation's capital. Princeton was the capital for just over four months, and Trenton had the honor for just over one month.

New Jersey became the third state to ratify the U.S. Constitution in 1787.

Two presidents had New Jersey connections. Grover Cleveland was born at Caldwell; however, he and his family moved away when he was a child. Woodrow Wilson was born in Virginia, but he moved to New Jersey and served as the president of Princeton University and Governor of New Jersey before his election as president.

Thomas Edison was another important person from New Jersey. Edison established his laboratory at Menlo Park. He demonstrated the first electric light at Menlo Park in 1879. He developed many other inventions there, including the motion picture and record player. Edison made his first motion pictures in New Jersey. The state was soon the location of the first major motion picture studios. Later, the studios moved to California to take advantage of better weather. The first drive-in movie theater opened near Camden in 1933.

Capital: Trenton
Nickname: The Garden State
Motto: Liberty and Prosperity
Major Cities: Newark, Patterson, Trenton
Population: 8,115,000 (est.)
Area: 7,700 square miles, 45th largest
Major Industries: Medicine, chemicals
Famous Citizens: Frank Sinatra, Meryl Streep, Stephen Crane
Flower: Purple Violet
Tree: Red Oak
Bird: Eastern Goldfinch

New Jersey became an industrial leader soon after becoming a state. Early industries included ironwork and glassmaking. Later industries included textiles and paper products. The state became a leading producer of ships and ammunition during the first half of the twentieth century. Today, New Jersey is a major producer of medicine, chemicals, and electronic equipment.

Tourism became important to the region in the early 1800s. The popularity of resort areas such as Atlantic City, continues. For many years, Atlantic City was the site of the annual Miss America Pageant.

Atlantic City was the basis for the game Monopoly®. The street names used in the game are real streets in Atlantic City.

Name: _____ Date: _____

Questions for Consideration

1. What is New Jersey's nickname?

   _____

2. Who were the first people to live in the New Jersey region?

   _____

3. Who claimed New Jersey for the Netherlands?

   _____

4. For what was New Jersey named?

   _____

5. What was one of the major battles of the Revolutionary War fought in New Jersey?

   _____

6. What were the New Jersey cities that served as the U.S. capital?

   _____

7. What president was born in New Jersey?

   _____

8. Who served as governor of New Jersey before becoming President of the United States?

   _____

9. What "first" happened near Camden in 1933?

   _____

10. What famous game uses the names of Atlantic City streets?

    _____

Activities

Topics for special reports:

Ammunition
Electric Lights
Woodrow Wilson
Phonograph
Thomas Edison
Washington's Crossing
    of the Delaware

Locate: On the map, put the number for each item in the proper location.

1. Atlantic Ocean
2. Delaware
3. Newark
4. New York
5. Pennsylvania
6. Trenton

NEW MEXICO

Scientists made a startling discovery in a New Mexico cave in 1990. They discovered tools over 55,000 years old. This is the earliest evidence of humans living in the entire Western Hemisphere.

Native American tribes continued to live in the region. Members of the Navajo, Apache, and Pueblo tribes met the first white explorers.

The Spanish were the first Europeans to explore the region. In 1536 Alvar Nuñez Cabeza de Vaca was probably the first white to explore New Mexico. Most of the early Spanish explorers were searching for gold.

Juan de Oñate claimed the region for Spain in 1598. The Spanish established San Juan Pueblo, the first permanent white settlement, in the same year.

In 1610, Santa Fe became the first capital of the territory. Santa Fe is the oldest capital in the United States. It became a capital ten years before the arrival of the Pilgrims.

When Mexico won independence from Spain in 1821, the New Mexico territory came under Mexico's control. During the Mexican War, General Stephen Kearny marched into Santa Fe and gained control of New Mexico for the United States.

New Mexico became a U.S. territory in 1850. The Gadsden Purchase of 1853 secured the rest of the current state.

New Mexico's most notorious citizen was William Bonney, better known as "Billy the Kid." According to legend, Billy the Kid killed 27 people before he was killed as the age of 21.

Friction between the settlers and the Native Americans and Mexicans continued. Apache raids ended in 1886 with the surrender of Geronimo. However, Pancho Villa, a Mexican outlaw, made several raids across the border in the 1910s.

New Mexico became the forty-seventh state in 1912.

Cattle and sheep ranching became major industries in the nineteenth century. Beef cattle and dairy herds are still the largest agricultural industries. New Mexico is the nation's largest producer of chili peppers.

New Mexico contains over 450 different minerals. Mining became the state's major industry. Prospectors found gold and silver in New Mexico in the middle of the nineteenth century. Today, copper and uranium are of major importance. The state also has large deposits of coal, natural gas, and petroleum.

During World War II, New Mexico became the site for secret research. In 1945, White Sands was the site of the first atomic bomb test. Later the government developed the first hydrogen bomb there. Just two years later a now-famous "flying saucer" incident occurred near Roswell. The incident still creates controversy. Witnesses state that they saw alien life, but the army and U.S. government deny the claims.

Capital: Santa Fe
Nickname: Land of Enchantment
Motto: It Grows as it Goes
Major Cities: Albuquerque, Santa Fe, Las Cruces
Population: 1,737,000 (est.)
Area: 121,500 square miles, 5th largest
Major Industries: Mining, agriculture
Famous Citizens: Billy the Kid, Conrad Hilton, Georgia O'Keefe, Lew Wallace
Flower: Yucca Flower
Tree: Piñon
Bird: Roadrunner

Name: _____ Date: _____

Questions for Consideration

1. What items over 55,000 years old did scientists discover in New Mexico?

   _____

2. Who were the first Europeans to visit New Mexico?

   _____

3. For what were they looking?

   _____

4. What was the name of the first permanent white settlement in New Mexico?

   _____

5. What is the oldest capital in the United States?

   _____

6. At the end of what war did the United States gain control over New Mexico?

   _____

7. Who was Pancho Villa?

   _____

8. What are the two most important minerals mined in New Mexico today?

   _____

9. Near what city was the first atomic bomb tested?

   _____

10. Where did a controversial "flying saucer" sighting occur?

    _____

Activities

Topics for special reports:

Apache Native Americans
Flying Saucers (UFOs)
William Bonney (Billy the Kid)
Geronimo
The Mexican War
Pancho Villa

Locate: On the map, put the number for each item in the proper location.

1. Albuquerque
2. Arizona
3. Colorado
4. Mexico
5. Santa Fe
6. Texas

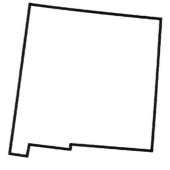

NEW YORK

New York is a state of many contrasts. It contains several row crop and dairy farms. It has numerous lakes and recreation areas. It also has many industrial centers and produces large quantities of concrete, chemicals, photography, and optical equipment. It is also home to New York City, one of the nation's major urban areas.

Members of the Algonquin and Iroquois tribes inhabited the New York region long before the arrival of the whites. During the French and Indian War, the Algonquins fought on the side of the French. Members of the Iroquois fought with the Americans and British.

Giovanni da Verrazano was the first European to see New York. He and his crew sailed into New York Harbor in 1524. Henry Hudson was English, but he sailed for the Dutch government in 1609 when he discovered the Hudson River. Like Columbus, Hudson was trying to find a passage to the Orient. Hudson claimed the land for the Netherlands. In 1625 the Dutch named the territory "New Netherlands." Nineteen years later, the British seized the territory and renamed it "New York." The name was in honor of the King of England's brother, the Duke of York.

During the Revolutionary War 92 battles were fought in New York. From 1785 to 1789, New York City was the nation's first capital. George Washington took his first oath of office as president there. In fact, Washington gave the state its nickname "the Empire State." While traveling through the state, he said that it was "the Seat of Empire."

A series of canals and roads helped New York become a major agricultural center. The most important of these, the Erie Canal, opened in 1825. Soon New York also developed into a major trade and industrial state. Banking, commerce, and transportation grew in importance after the Civil War. Today, New York is also the center of the nation's communication and financial industries.

Five presidents have New York associations. Martin Van Buren, Millard Fillmore, Theodore Roosevelt, and Franklin D. Roosevelt were all born in the state. Grover Cleveland was born in New Jersey but moved to New York as a child.

Capital: Albany
Nickname: The Empire State
Motto: Ever Upward
Major Cities: Albany, Buffalo, New York City, Rochester, Syracuse
Population: 18,175,000 (est.)
Area: 49,100 square miles, 30th largest
Major Industries: Financial, film, clothing
Famous Citizens: Franklin D. Roosevelt, Theodore Roosevelt, Mickey Mantle, J. P. Morgan
Flower: Rose
Tree: Sugar Maple
Bird: Bluebird

New York City has always been of major importance to the state. Originally named "New Amsterdam" by the Dutch, it became New York City when the English gained control. By the middle of the nineteenth century, it became the world's largest city. Between the 1890s and 1920s, Ellis Island was the entry port of over 17 million immigrants. New York City is the site of many important structures including the Brooklyn Bridge (1883), the Statue of Liberty (1886), the Empire State Building (1931), and the United Nations Headquarters (1952).

Tragedy struck New York City on September 11, 2001, when Al Qaeda terrorists hijacked two airliners and crashed them into the two towers of the World Trade Center. The towers burned and collapsed, killing 2,749 people. Two more airliners were hijacked that day. One crashed in Pennsylvania, and the other one struck the Pentagon building, killing an additional 225 people.

Name: _____ Date: _____

Questions for Consideration

1. What two major Native American nations lived in New York?

   _____

2. What English explorer, sailing for the Dutch, claimed New York?

   _____

3. For whom was New York named?

   _____

4. How many Revolutionary War battles took place in New York?

   _____

5. Where did George Washington take his first oath of office as president?

   _____

6. What nickname did George Washington give New York?

   _____

7. What famous canal opened in New York in 1825?

   _____

8. How many Presidents of the United States were born in New York?

   _____

9. What was the Dutch name for New York City?

   _____

10. What terrorist organization was responsible for the September 11, 2001, attacks?

   _____

Activities

Topics for special reports:

Empire State Building
Erie Canal
Iroquois Native Americans
New York City
Statue of Liberty
One of the presidents
    from New York

Locate: On the map, put the number for each item in the proper location.

1. Albany
2. Atlantic Ocean
3. Lake Erie
4. Lake Ontario
5. Pennsylvania
6. Connecticut
7. New York City

NORTH CAROLINA

Many North Carolina names come from English sources. The name "Carolina" is from the Latin name for Charles. The state's name honors King Charles I of England. The state's capital, Raleigh, honors the English explorer Sir Walter Raleigh. North Carolina's largest city, Charlotte, honors Queen Charlotte, the wife of King George III.

Explorers representing France and Spain were the earliest Europeans to visit the region. However, the first settlers were English. Sir Walter Raleigh founded the first English settlement, Roanoke, in 1585. This colony failed and Raleigh returned to England.

The English founded a second colony, also named Roanoke, two years later. One month after the establishment of the second Roanoke colony, Virginia Dare became the first English child born in America. The leader of the colony, Governor White, soon had to return to England for supplies. He was unable to return for three years. When he did return, he found no trace of any of the colonists. He found the word "Croatoan" carved on a tree. The Croatoans were a tribe of Native Americans living in the region. No one knows what happened to the settlers of Roanoke, the "Lost Colony."

North and South Carolina were originally one territory. The division into two territories occurred in 1712. President Andrew Jackson was born near the border of the two states. Today, both states claim to be his birthplace. Presidents James Polk and Andrew Johnson were born in North Carolina. First Lady Dolley Madison is another North Carolina native.

Pirates roamed the coast of the Carolinas. The most notorious of the group was Blackbeard. He prowled the region until his death in 1718 near Ocracoke Inlet. The two most infamous female pirates, Anne Bonney and Mary Read, also had headquarters in the region.

North Carolina was the first colony to officially declare its willingness to fight for independence from England. The Revolutionary War battle of Moore's Creek Bridge was on February 22, 1776. In 1789, North Carolina became the twelfth state to ratify the U.S. Constitution.

North Carolina seceded from the Union in 1861. Over 100 Civil War battles were fought in North Carolina. Major battles fought in the state include Averasboro, Bentonville, and Durham Station. North Carolina rejoined the Union in 1868.

Kitty Hawk became the site of the first powered airplane flight. The Wright Brothers made their famous flight there in 1903.

The major recreational area of the state is the Great Smoky Mountains National Park established in 1934. The park includes hiking trails, over 1,500 species of plants, and several "living museums" showing pioneer life.

Early agricultural crops of the state were cotton and tobacco. Industrialization did not begin until the 1880s. Textiles, tobacco, and furniture continue to be the state's major products. In recent years, North Carolina has become a major location of electronics and medicine production as well as technological research.

Capital: Raleigh
Nickname: The Tar Heel State
Motto: To Be Rather Than to Seem
Major Cities: Charlotte, Greensboro, Raleigh, Winston-Salem
Population: 7,546,000 (est.)
Area: 52,600 square miles, 28th largest
Major Industries: Tobacco, medicine, electronics, furniture
Famous Citizens: Billy Graham, Andy Griffith, Randy Travis, Michael Jordan
Flower: Flowering Dogwood
Tree: Pine
Bird: Cardinal

Name: _____ Date: _____

Questions for Consideration

1. Who does the name "Carolina" honor?

   _____

2. Who founded the first English settlement in North Carolina?

   _____

3. What was the name of this settlement?

   _____

4. Who was the first English child born in America?

   _____

5. What famous first lady was born in North Carolina?

   _____

6. Who was the most notorious pirate to live in North Carolina?

   _____

7. What Revolutionary War battle occurred in North Carolina on February 22, 1776?

   _____

8. What was the site of the Wright Brothers' famous flight?

   _____

9. What major recreational area was established in North Carolina in 1934?

   _____

10. What were the two major agricultural crops in North Carolina's early history?

   _____

Activities

Topics for special reports:

Andrew Johnson
Dolley Madison
Pirates
Sir Walter Raleigh
Tobacco
Wright Brothers

Locate: On the map, put the number for each item in the proper location.

1. Atlantic Ocean
2. Charlotte
3. Raleigh
4. Tennessee
5. Winston-Salem
6. Virginia

NORTH DAKOTA

In prehistoric ages, a series of glaciers moved across the land that is now North Dakota. The glaciers created a flat barren land. The temperature differences between summers and winters are the most extreme of any state in the nation. These conditions discouraged early settlement of the region.

The earliest inhabitants of the region were nomadic tribes. The Mandans settled in the region over 600 years ago. Other tribes to hunt and later settle in the region included the other Sioux tribes, the Arikara, Cheyenne, Hidasta, and Ojibwa.

The word *Dakota* comes from the name of one of the Sioux Native American tribes. It means "allies" or "friends."

La Salle claimed the region for France in 1682. However, it was not until 1738 that the first Europeans traveled into the region. Fur traders soon established friendly relations with the natives. A permanent trading post began operating in 1801.

The territory was part of the Louisiana Purchase. The Lewis and Clark Expedition entered the state in October 1804. They built a winter camp, which they named Ft. Mandan, on the Missouri River near the present site of Bismarck. The expedition left the fort to continue its journey in April 1805. They hired Toussaint Charbonneau to be an interpreter. Toussaint's wife, Sacajawea, and their infant son joined the expedition. Sacajawea served as guide and translator. Today, a statue on the capitol grounds at Bismarck honors Sacajawea.

The first permanent white settlement began in 1812. Because of the harsh climate, population growth was slow. The territory opened to homesteaders in 1863. Most of the early settlers were German and Norwegian. Settlers arrived from other Scandinavian countries and Canada. Settlement increased significantly with the arrival of the first railroad to enter the state in 1871.

Oliver Dalrymple began the "bonanza" farm idea in 1876. Under Dalrymple's plan, groups of farmers worked together to grow a crop on thousands of acres of land. This plan worked well on the vast open acres of North Dakota. The bonanza farms also helped increase the territory's population.

Capital: Bismarck

Nicknames: The Flickertail State, Peace Garden State

Motto: Liberty and Union, Now and Forever, One and Inseparable

Major Cities: Bismarck, Fargo, Grand Forks

Population: 638,000 (est.)

Area: 70,700 square miles, 17th largest

Major Industries: Agriculture, mining

Famous Citizens: Roger Maris, Lawrence Welk, Louis L'Amour

Flower: Wild Prairie Rose

Tree: American Elm

Bird: Western Meadowlark

North Dakota became a state on November 2, 1889. This was the same day that South Dakota received statehood. When President Benjamin Harrison signed the statehood documents for the two states, he deliberately shuffled the papers so he wouldn't know which one he signed first. He did this so critics could not accuse him of favoritism. Officially North Dakota is the thirty-ninth and South Dakota the fortieth state because of alphabetical order.

Agriculture remains the state's major industry. Major products include wheat, barley, sunflowers, and cattle. Mining is the second largest industry. The nation's largest coal reserves are in North Dakota. Geologists found a major oil reserve in the state in 1951. Today, the state produces a significant part of the nation's crude oil supply.

Name: _____ Date: _____

Questions for Consideration

1. Why is North Dakota so flat?

   _____

2. What Native American tribe settled in what is now North Dakota over 600 years ago?

   _____

3. What does the Sioux word *Dakota* mean?

   _____

4. When did traders establish the first trading post in North Dakota?

   _____

5. What did Lewis and Clark name the fort they built in North Dakota?

   _____

6. What woman is honored with a statue on North Dakota's capitol grounds?

   _____

7. What was the name of the farm idea created by Oliver Dalrymple?

   _____

8. What president signed the papers making North Dakota a state?

   _____

9. Why is North Dakota the thirty-ninth instead of the fortieth state?

   _____

10. What natural resource was discovered in North Dakota in 1951?

    _____

Activities

Topics for special reports:

Glaciers
Sioux Native Americans
Mandan Native Americans
Sacajawea

Locate: On the map, put the number for each item in the proper location.

1. Bismarck
2. Canada
3. Fargo
4. Minnesota
5. Montana
6. Red River

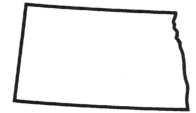

OHIO

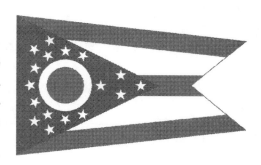

One of the earliest groups to inhabit Ohio were the Mound Builders. Many of these mounds still exist in the state. The most famous is the Serpent Mound near Locust Grove. The mound is one fourth of a mile long and, at some points, five feet high.

Later Native American tribes to live in the region included the Delaware, Erie, Huron, Iroquois, Miami, Ottawa, Shawnee, and Tuscarora.

Ohio is an Iroquois word meaning "something great" or "great river." The Ohio River is one of the nation's most important waterways. It begins in Pennsylvania and empties into the Mississippi River. The Ohio River became one of the most important transportation links between the East and Midwest. Many settlers used the river during their westward migration. They also used the river to ship goods and produce to eastern markets.

The first European to visit Ohio was either La Salle or Joliet. Both of these Frenchmen traveled in the region in 1669. Both the French and English governments claimed the territory. Who controlled Ohio became one of the issues that caused the French and Indian War. The 1763 Treaty of Paris gave the territory to England. The region came under U.S. control after the Revolutionary War.

Settlers soon moved into the Ohio region. They established Marietta, the first permanent white settlement. Ohio became the seventeenth state in 1803. The rapid increase in population continued. It soon became a major agricultural, trade, and industrial center. The opening of the Ohio and Erie Canals in 1832 and several railroads aided the region's rapid growth.

Ohio has three interesting nicknames. The most common is "the Buckeye State." The buckeye is a tree that grew well in the region. Pioneers made many useful items from buckeyes.

One of Ohio's other nicknames is the "Mother of Presidents." Ohio is the birthplace of seven United States presidents. Rutherford B. Hayes, Warren G. Harding, James A. Garfield, William McKinley, Ulysses S. Grant, William Henry Harrison, and William Howard Taft were Ohio natives.

A third nickname for the state is "Mother of Invention." The most famous Ohio-born inventors include Thomas Edison and the Wright Brothers. Edison moved to New Jersey where he carried out his experiments. The Wright Brothers developed their flying machine in their bicycle shop in Dayton. Other Ohio inventors include B. F. Goodrich (vulcanized rubber) and R. E. Olds (founder of the Oldsmobile automobile company).

Ohio is still an important agricultural center. Major crops include soybeans and corn. It is also a major provider of dairy products.

Ohio is the birthplace of John Glenn, Jr. Glenn was the first American in orbit. He later became a senator for Ohio. Glenn made another important contribution to space exploration when in 1998, at the age of 77, he joined a space shuttle mission.

Capital: Columbus
Nickname: The Buckeye State
Motto: With God, All Things are Possible
Major Cities: Akron, Cleveland, Cincinnati, Columbus, Toledo, Dayton
Population: 11,209,000 (est.)
Area: 41,300 square miles, 35th largest
Major Industries: Agriculture, machinery, coal
Famous Citizens: John Glenn, Jr., Steven Spielberg, the Wright Brothers, Thomas Edison, Neil Armstrong
Flower: Scarlet Carnation
Tree: Buckeye
Bird: Cardinal

Name: _____ Date: _____

Questions for Consideration

1. What is the most famous mound in Ohio?

   _____

2. What did the Iroquois word *Ohio* mean?

   _____

3. Into what river does the Ohio River empty?

   _____

4. What was the first permanent white settlement in Ohio?

   _____

5. What two canals helped Ohio's rapid growth?

   _____

6. What is a buckeye?

   _____

7. Ohio is the birthplace of how many U.S. presidents?

   _____

8. In what Ohio town did the Wright Brothers develop their flying machine?

   _____

9. What Ohio native invented vulcanized rubber?

   _____

10. What former astronaut became a U.S. senator representing Ohio?

   _____

Activities

Topics for special reports:

French and Indian War
One of the presidents
   born in Ohio
Ohio River
Rubber
John Glenn, Jr.
Neil Armstrong

Locate: On the map, put the number for each item in the proper location.

1. Cincinnati
2. Columbus
3. Dayton
4. Indiana
5. Ohio River
6. Pennsylvania
7. West Virginia

OKLAHOMA

The earliest humans to live in what is now Oklahoma were members of the Clovis group. They lived over 11,000 years ago. The Folsom Culture arrived over 10,000 years ago. The Plano Culture arrived next, followed by the Mound Builders who arrived about 3,000 years ago. Artifacts of all these cultures remain in the state.

Members of the Apache, Caddo, Comanche, Kiowa, Pawnee, Osage, and Quapaw tribes lived in the region when the first European explorers arrived. Later tribes to move into the region included the Cherokee, Choctaw, Chickasaw, Creek, and Seminole. The name *Oklahoma* comes from Choctaw words meaning "red man" or "land of red men."

By the early 1800s, the U.S. government began moving Native Americans living east of the Mississippi River into the Indian Territory of Oklahoma. The government forced the move of members of over 60 tribes. The most infamous of these migrations was the "Trail of Tears" movement of the Cherokees.

In 1541, the Spanish explorer Francisco Vasquez de Coronado was the first European to visit the region. La Salle claimed the region for France in 1682. Both France and Spain claimed the region. It came under the control of the United States as part of the Louisiana Purchase.

Originally, the U.S. government set aside the Oklahoma Territory for Native Americans. However, pressure from the railroads and settlers forced the government to open the region for white settlers. The government bought some land from the Native American tribes and allowed whites to have up to 160 acres of land free, if they agreed to live on the land and farm it. Major land rushes occurred in 1889 and 1893. The largest land rush occurred in September 1893. Over 100,000 settlers lined up at the Kansas-Oklahoma border to race to make land claims. Cities grew overnight. Oklahoma City had a population of 10,000 and Guthrie grew to 15,000 in just one day.

Many settlers moved in ahead of the official signal to stake their claims. They became known as "sooners." One of Oklahoma's nicknames is "the Sooner State."

Oklahoma became the forty-sixth state in 1907.

Farming and livestock became the state's major industries. Major crops include peanuts, cotton, and wheat. At first, there was much friction between the farmers and the ranchers. The Rogers and Hammerstein musical *Oklahoma!* deals with this conflict.

Poor farming practices and a long drought plagued the state in the 1930s. The region became known as "the Dust Bowl." Many farmers lost their lands and had to move to other states. Many became migrant workers. John Steinbeck's famous novel *The Grapes of Wrath* tells about one family of the time.

Oklahoma has many important natural resources. Drillers discovered oil in 1859. Oklahoma also contains large deposits of natural gas and coal.

Oklahoma City, the state's capital, became the site of tragedy when a bomb destroyed the Federal Building and killed 168 people in 1995.

Capital: Oklahoma City
Nickname: The Sooner State
Motto: Labor Conquers All Things
Major Cities: Lawton, Norman, Oklahoma City, Tulsa
Population: 3,347,000 (est.)
Area: 69,900 square miles, 18th largest
Major Industries: Oil, agriculture
Famous Citizen: Will Rogers, Jim Thorpe, Johnny Bench
Flower: Mistletoe
Tree: Redbud
Bird: Scissor-tailed Flycatcher

Name: _____ Date: _____

Questions for Consideration

1. Members of what culture lived in what is now Oklahoma over 11,000 years ago?

   _____

2. What does the Choctaw word *Oklahoma* mean?

   _____

3. What is the name of the forced migration of the Cherokees into Oklahoma?

   _____

4. What two European nations claimed the Oklahoma region?

   _____

5. How many acres of land could someone have if they agreed to farm it?

   _____

6. What name was given to settlers who moved into the territory ahead of the signal?

   _____

7. What Broadway musical dealt with the conflict between farmers and ranchers?

   _____

8. What did the Oklahoma region become known as in the 1930s?

   _____

9. What famous novel told the story of migrant workers in the 1930s?

   _____

10. In what year did a bomb destroy the Federal Building in Oklahoma City?

   _____

Activities

Topics for special reports:

Choctaw Native Americans
The Dust Bowl
Migrant Workers
The Trail of Tears
Oklahoma Land Rush

Locate: On the map, put the number for each item in the proper location.

1. Arkansas
2. Kansas
3. Oklahoma City
4. Red River
5. Texas
6. Tulsa

OREGON

The Cascade Mountain Range runs north and south through Oregon. The region west of the mountains receives large amounts of rainfall from storms off the Pacific coast. The mountains prevent the clouds from moving into the rest of the state. Thus, eastern Oregon is much drier and has colder winters and hotter summers.

Many ships explored the coast of Oregon before any exploration of the interior began. In 1792, Robert Gray explored and named the Columbia River.

The Lewis and Clark Expedition explored the region in 1805 and 1806. They reached the mouth of the Columbia River in November 1805. They established a camp named Fort Clatsop to spend the winter months. Their stay at the camp was miserable. They suffered through cold, rain, and hunger. They left their camp in April 1806 to begin their trip home.

British and French fur trappers and traders soon moved into the region. The state received its nickname "The Beaver State" from the large number of beaver skins sent to the East to make hats and clothing trim. John Jacob Astor's American Fur Company established a trading post in 1811. The settlement was named Astoria in his honor.

Thousands of settlers began traveling on the 2,000-mile-long Oregon Trail in 1841. They settled in what is now Oregon, Washington, and Idaho.

The U.S. government established the Oregon Territory in 1848. The Donation Land Law of 1850 encouraged settlement. According to the law, a man and his wife could claim 640 acres of free land if they settled in the region.

The discovery of gold in the region in 1850 also encouraged settlement. Oregon became the thirty-third state in 1859.

Lumber and wood products remain Oregon's major industries. To help maintain the forests, a law now requires the lumber industry to plant a new tree for each one that it cuts. Logging is not permitted on over two million acres of the state. In recent years, controversy has increased about the lumber industry. Many environmentalists oppose the clearing of any new forests especially those with older trees.

Capital: Salem
Nickname: The Beaver State
Motto: She Flies With Her Own Wings
Major Cities: Eugene, Portland, Salem
Population: 3,282,000 (est.)
Area: 97,000 square miles, 10th largest
Major Industries: Lumber, wood products, agriculture
Famous Citizens: John Reed, Doc Severinsen, Linus Pauling
Flower: Oregon Grape
Tree: Douglas Fir
Bird: Western Meadowlark

Even though the state has little farm land, it still produces significant crops of wheat, cranberries, apples, pears, cherries, and peppermint. Oregon also maintains a large cattle and dairy industry.

From the state's earliest years, fishing has been a major industry. Salmon, tuna, flounder, oysters, and sturgeon all contribute to the state's fishing industry.

Early in its history, Portland was a shipping and transportation center. It became a major ship building center during both World War I and World War II. During World War II, Portland launched over 1,000 ocean-going ships.

Oregon has a wide range of recreational facilities available. It contains 110 recreational areas and wildlife refuges. It also has 13 national forests and over 200 state parks.

Name: _____ Date: _____

Questions for Consideration

1. What mountain range runs through Oregon?

    _____

2. What river did Robert Gray name?

    _____

3. What did Lewis and Clark name their winter camp?

    _____

4. For whom was Astoria named?

    _____

5. When did the Oregon Trail begin?

    _____

6. What did the Donation Land Law promise each man and his wife?

    _____

7. What 1850 event helped encourage settlement of Oregon?

    _____

8. When did Oregon become a state?

    _____

9. What Oregon industry has created major controversies in recent years?

    _____

10. How many ocean-going ships were built in Portland during World War II?

    _____

Activities

Topics for special reports:

Fishing Industry
Lumber Industry
Homesteading
Lewis and Clark in
   Oregon

Locate: On the map, put the number for each item in the proper location.

1. Astoria
2. California
3. Columbia River
4. Pacific Ocean
5. Portland
6. Washington
7. Salem

PENNSYLVANIA

Early in its history, English, Dutch, and Swedes all claimed the land that is now Pennsylvania. Henry Hudson may have explored the region in 1609. Other Dutch sailors explored the Delaware River and the land along its shores by 1614. The Swedes, led by Johan Prinz, established a village on Tinicum Island in 1643. The British claimed the region in 1664. England's King Charles II gave William Penn 28 million acres of land in America in 1681. The king did this to pay a debt owed to Penn's father. The name *Pennsylvania* means "Penn's woods" in Latin.

The following year, Penn established a colony in the New World. Penn was a Quaker. To avoid persecution in England, Penn and his fellow Quakers established the colony on the basis of religious freedom. They named their colony "Philadelphia." The name came from a Greek term meaning "city of brotherly love."

German settlers soon moved into the region in the late 1600s. They began farming the land. Agriculture has always been an important part of the state's economy. Cattle and dairy products remain a major industry.

Much of the movement for American independence occurred in Pennsylvania. Citizens began to speak out against the British as early as 1766.

Philadelphia was of major importance during the Revolutionary War. It became the site of the First and Second Continental Congresses. Representatives of the colonies signed the Declaration of Independence in Philadelphia in July 1776. The signing of the U.S. Constitution also occurred there. In addition to Independence Hall and the Liberty Bell, the city is the site of the Betsy Ross House, Carpenter's Hall, and the grave of Benjamin Franklin.

George Washington and his troops survived a bitter winter at Valley Forge in 1777.

Pennsylvania became the second state to ratify the Constitution. Philadelphia was the nation's capital from 1790 until the government moved the capital to Washington, D.C., in 1800.

Philadelphia became a center of shipbuilding during the War of 1812. Carpenters built many ships to help keep control of the Great Lakes. They built Commodore Oliver Hazard Perry's ship, *Niagara*. During the battle of Lake Erie, Perry used his now famous saying, "Don't give up the ship."

Pennsylvania soon became the industrial center of the nation. Pioneers built the first iron forge near Pottstown in 1716. They made the first steel in 1732. Canals and later railroads helped ship both raw materials and finished goods. Iron and coal grew into major industries before the Civil War. The world's first oil well was drilled near Titusville. By the mid-1800s, Pittsburgh became the nation's major steel producer.

During the Civil War, Pennsylvania remained in the Union. One of that war's greatest battles, the Battle of Gettysburg, took place on Pennsylvania soil.

Pennsylvania is the chocolate capital of the nation. Milton Hershey developed a process that allowed chocolate candy to remain fresh longer. His factory in the town of Hershey still produces much of the nation's chocolate supply.

Capital: Harrisburg
Nickname: The Keystone State
Motto: Virtue, Liberty, and Independence
Major Cities: Erie, Philadelphia, Pittsburgh
Population: 12,001,000 (est.)
Area: 45,300 square miles, 33rd largest
Major Industries: Agriculture, mining, metal products
Famous Citizen: Benjamin Franklin
Flower: Mountain Laurel
Tree: Eastern Hemlock
Bird: Ruffed Grouse

76

Name: _____ Date: _____

Questions for Consideration

1. What noted explorer may have visited Pennsylvania in 1609?

   _____

2. What does *Pennsylvania* mean?

   _____

3. What does *Philadelphia* mean?

   _____

4. What are Pennsylvania's major agricultural products?

   _____

5. Where did George Washington and his men spend the winter of 1777?

   _____

6. What was Commodore Perry's most famous quotation?

   _____

7. What was built near Pottstown in 1716?

   _____

8. Where was the first oil well drilled?

   _____

9. What important Civil War battle happened in Pennsylvania?

   _____

10. Who developed a process to preserve chocolate candy?

   _____

Activities

Topics for special reports:

Chocolate
Commodore Perry
Philadelphia
Quakers
Betsy Ross
Steel

Locate: On the map, put the number for each item in the proper location.

1. Harrisburg
2. Lake Erie
3. New York
4. Ohio
5. Philadelphia
6. Pittsburgh

RHODE ISLAND

Rhode Island is the smallest state. It is 37 miles wide from east to west and 48 miles wide from north to south. In spite of its name, it is not an island. However, its Atlantic Ocean coast contains 36 islands. The largest of these had the Native American name "Aquidneck."

An early Italian explorer, Giovanni da Verrazano, may have renamed the island Aquidneck, Rhode Island, after the Isle of Rhodes in the Aegean Sea. Another legend is that the state's name comes from the Dutch words *Roodt Eyalandt* meaning "red island."

Roger Williams founded the first white settlement in Rhode Island in 1636. Williams left England in search of religious freedom. At first, he lived in Massachusetts with the Pilgrims, but they did not approve of anyone who disagreed with them. The governor of Massachusetts ordered Williams to return to England. Instead, he and some of his friends fled to Rhode Island.

The group established good relations with the Native Americans in the region. They bought their land from the Algonquins. With the help of Chief Massasoit, the settlers survived their early difficulties. They named their new settlement Providence.

Williams provided the same religious freedom to others that he achieved for his followers. Many other groups came into the region for this religious freedom and protection. The state is the location of the nation's oldest Quaker Meeting House built at Newport in 1669. Newport is also the site of the country's oldest Jewish synagogue built in 1763. The first Baptist Church in America, founded in 1638, is in Providence.

Rhode Islanders carried on major trade with the British. When the British began to put restrictions and taxes on trade, Rhode Islanders protested by burning a British ship in 1772.

Rhode Island declared its independence from the British on May 4, 1776. It became the site of many battles during the Revolutionary War. The British captured Newport and burned many of its buildings. Rhode Island furnished many soldiers for the American cause. Nathanael Greene became Washington's second-in-command. Esek Hopkins became commander-in-chief of the Continental Navy.

The first colony to declare its independence, it was the last to ratify the Constitution. In 1790, Rhode Island became the thirteenth state.

Capital: Providence
Nickname: Little Rhody and The Ocean State
Motto: Hope
Major Cities: Warwick, Providence, Newport
Population: 988,000 (est.)
Area: 1,200 square miles, the smallest
Major Industries: Textiles, jewelry
Famous Citizens: Nathanael Greene, George M. Cohan, Gilbert Stuart
Flower: Violet
Tree: Red Maple
Bird: Rhode Island Red

Agriculture began early in the state's history. Shipbuilding and whaling were also of early importance. The state later became the home to two major industries: textiles and jewelry. It was the location of the nation's first cotton mill in 1790. Today, it is still one of the nation's major producers of silverware.

In the late nineteenth century, many wealthy families built summer homes in Newport. Though they called them "cottages," they were really large mansions. The most famous of these is the Breakers, built by the Vanderbilt family in 1892.

For many years, Rhode Island farmers were noted for raising chickens. In 1895 the "Rhode Island Red" became recognized as a new breed. It is now officially the state bird.

Name: _____ Date: _____

Questions for Consideration

1. What do the Dutch words *Roodt Eyalandt* mean?

   _____

2. Who founded the first white settlement in Rhode Island?

   _____

3. What did they name their settlement?

   _____

4. When was the nation's first synagogue built?

   _____

5. What British possession did Rhode Island citizens burn in 1772?

   _____

6. What Rhode Island town did the British burn during the Revolutionary War?

   _____

7. What Rhode Island native became George Washington's second-in-command?

   _____

8. What "first" was built in Rhode Island in 1790?

   _____

9. What is Rhode Island's state bird?

   _____

10. In what Rhode Island city did many wealthy families build their summer "cottages"?

    _____

Activities

Topics for special reports:

Chickens (poultry)
Nathanael Greene
Silverware
Roger Williams

Locate: On the map, put the number for each item in the proper location.

1. Atlantic Ocean
2. Connecticut
3. Massachusetts
4. Newport
5. Providence

SOUTH CAROLINA

Humans have inhabited South Carolina for over 11,000 years. The earliest were hunters and gatherers. Later, tribes settled in the region and agriculture began. When the first Europeans arrived, over 20,000 natives lived in the area.

Native Americans included tribes from the Iroquois, Sioux, and Muskogean families. Tribes included the Catawbas, Cherokees, Congarees, Coosas, Cusabos, Kiawahs, Westros, and Yamasees. Almost all of the tribes moved westward out of the state by 1800.

Spanish explorers were the first Europeans to visit the region. A group led by Francisco Gordillo explored the region in 1521. The Spanish established a settlement in 1526, but it failed in less than a year. French settlers tried to establish a colony in 1562, but it also failed. Hunger and disease plagued both settlements.

King Charles I gave a land grant to a group of eight men to establish a colony in the new world. The grant included land that later became North Carolina, South Carolina, and part of Georgia. The name *Carolina* honored King Charles I. It came from the Latin name for "Charles." The English made the first permanent white settlement, named Charles Towne, in 1670. They also named the settlement in honor of their king. Later, settlers shortened its name to Charleston. North and South Carolina became separate colonies in 1729.

Pirates sailed along the coasts of South Carolina and its neighboring states. Blackbeard was the most notorious of them. The governors of South Carolina and Virginia formed a group to fight the pirates. They killed Blackbeard in a battle off the coast of North Carolina.

Friction soon developed between the colonists and the British, and the state became involved in the Revolutionary War. South Carolina received its nickname "the Palmetto State" during the war. Colonists built Fort Moultrie out of palmetto logs to defend Charleston from the British. The colonists defended the area, destroyed a British warship, and won the battle. More battles of the Revolutionary War occurred in South Carolina than in any other state.

On May 23, 1788, South Carolina became the eighth state to join the Union.

South Carolina became the first state to leave the Union prior to the Civil War. It seceded in December 1860. In April 1861, the Confederates fired on Fort Sumter in Charleston Harbor to start the war.

Early South Carolina crops included rice and indigo. Indigo is a plant used in the manufacturing of blue dye. Later, cotton became the major crop. South Carolina soon became a major producer of textiles. The textile industry is still of great importance to the state's economy.

Today, other industries include chemicals, paper products, and agriculture. While cotton is still important, tobacco and soybeans have passed cotton as the major crop. Tourism has increased in recent years. South Carolina's beaches are major recreation areas. Myrtle Beach and Hilton Head Island are the sites of many resorts and notable golf courses.

Capital: Columbia
Nickname: The Palmetto State
Motto: While I Breathe, I Hope
Major Cities: Charleston, Columbia
Population: 3,836,000 (est.)
Area: 31,100 square miles, 40th largest
Major Industries: Agriculture, chemicals, paper products
Famous Citizens: John C. Calhoun, Joe Frazier, Jesse Jackson
Flower: Yellow Jessamine
Tree: Palmetto
Bird: Carolina Wren

Name: _____ Date: _____

Questions for Consideration

1. Who was the first European explorer of what is now South Carolina?

_____

2. For whom was South Carolina named?

_____

3. What was the original name of Charleston?

_____

4. What pirate did the governor of South Carolina help defeat?

_____

5. What is South Carolina's nickname?

_____

6. What was the name of the fort that Confederates fired on to start the Civil War?

_____

7. What is made from indigo?

_____

8. What became South Carolina's major crop and led to the state's textile industry?

_____

9. What are South Carolina's two major crops today?

_____

10. What are the two most noted locations of resorts and golf courses in South Carolina?

_____

Activities

Topics for special reports:

Blackbeard
Charleston
Fort Sumter
Indigo
Palmetto

Locate: On the map, put the number for each item in the proper location.

1. Atlantic Ocean
2. Charleston
3. Columbia
4. Georgia
5. Hilton Head
6. Myrtle Beach

SOUTH DAKOTA

The name *Dakota* came from the Dakota or Sioux Native Americans. The name means "friends" or "allies." Humans may have inhabited the region for over 25,000 years. Tribes living in the region when the first Europeans arrived included the Mandan, Hidatsa, and Sioux.

The earliest Europeans to explore the region were brothers Louis Joseph and François La Vérendrye. They claimed the territory for France. France ceded the territory to Spain in 1762. France regained the territory before selling it to the United States as part of the Louisiana Purchase of 1803. Congress established the Dakota Territory in 1861. The territory included both North and South Dakota. Population of the new territory grew slowly. Railroads reached the region in 1871. The discovery of gold in 1874 caused an increase of population in the region. Both North Dakota and South Dakota became states in 1889. North Dakota was the thirty-ninth and South Dakota the fortieth state.

The Lewis and Clark Expedition explored parts of the region during the trip westward in 1804 and on the return trip in 1806. Fur trappers and traders began to move into the region. The government built Fort Pierre as a trading post in 1817.

Tensions between the Native Americans and the settlers increased. The Battle of the Little Big Horn occurred in neighboring Montana in 1876. The chief of the Sioux, Sitting Bull, surrendered at Fort Buford in 1881. The Battle of Wounded Knee was in 1890. This was the last major battle between the federal troops and Native Americans.

Agriculture remains one of South Dakota's major industries. Livestock, mainly cattle and hogs, and livestock products make up two-thirds of the state's agricultural economy. Corn, wheat, oats, and rye are major crops.

Gold mining continues as a major industry. The Homestake Mine, located in the Black Hills, is the largest underground gold mine in the Western Hemisphere. Geologists discovered uranium in the state in 1951 and plutonium in 1952. South Dakota is also the major producer of the clay bentonite. Foundries as well as the oil drilling, insulation, and chemical industries all use bentonite.

South Dakota contains many tourist attractions. The most famous is Mount Rushmore. Sculptor Gutzon Borglum and his son supervised over 300 workers on the monument from 1927 until 1941. The giant sculpture, carved into a mountainside, includes the faces of George Washington, Thomas Jefferson, Abraham Lincoln, and Theodore Roosevelt. The faces are between 60 and 70 feet tall. Another large sculpture, one of Chief Crazy Horse, is currently being carved 17 miles from Mount Rushmore.

Another popular attraction is the region of the Badlands. Here, over time, the wind and water carved many interesting forms out of the barren wasteland.

The restored mining town of Deadwood is a reminder of South Dakota's Wild West history. Its cemetery contains the graves of Wild Bill Hickok and Calamity Jane.

Capital: Pierre
Nickname: Coyote State
Motto: Under God the People Rule
Major Cities: Pierre, Rapid City, Sioux Falls
Population: 738,000 (est.)
Area: 77,100 square miles, 16th largest
Major Industries: Agriculture, mining
Famous Citizens: George McGovern, Tom Brokaw, Mary Hart
Flower: Pasqueflower
Tree: Black Hills Spruce
Bird: Ring-necked Pheasant

Name: _____ Date: _____

Questions for Consideration

1. What does the name *Dakota* mean?

   _____

2. What was the name of the first trading post in South Dakota?

   _____

3. What other territory became a state at the same time as South Dakota?

   _____

4. Where did Chief Sitting Bull surrender?

   _____

5. What is the largest underground gold mine in South Dakota?

   _____

6. What did geologists discover in South Dakota in 1951?

   _____

7. What is bentonite?

   _____

8. What famous South Dakota monument honors four presidents?

   _____

9. Who is being honored by another large sculpture that is still being carved?

   _____

10. What famous woman is buried in Deadwood's cemetery?

   _____

Activities

Topics for special reports:

The Badlands
Gold Mining
Mount Rushmore
Wild Bill Hickok
Chief Sitting Bull

Locate: On the map, put the number for each item in the proper location.

1. Iowa
2. Minnesota
3. North Dakota
4. Nebraska
5. Pierre
6. Sioux Falls

TENNESSEE

The first humans to live in what is now Tennessee were Paleo-Indians. Later civilizations included the Archaic, Woodland, Mississippian, and the Mound Builders. Tribes living in the area when the first Europeans arrived included the Cherokee, Chickasaw, Chickamonga, Creek, Shawnee, and Yuchi.

Tennessee possibly got its name from the Cherokee word *Tanasie. Tanasie* was the name of a river and Cherokee village.

In 1540, Hernando de Soto and his men were the first Europeans to visit the region. He claimed the region for Spain. The Spaniards built a fort in 1566. The French explorers Marquette and Joliet visited the region in 1673. French and British traders entered the area in the late 1600s. The French built a trading post named French Lick in 1714. French Lick was near the present location of Nashville. The British came into complete control of the land after winning the French and Indian War in 1763.

Settlers from the East began to enter the region through the Cumberland Gap on the Wilderness Road established by Daniel Boone. A number of noted frontier pioneers including Davy Crockett and Sam Houston lived or were born in the state.

From 1784 to 1787, settlers in the eastern part of the region established the State of Franklin, named for Benjamin Franklin. The federal government never recognized the independence of the territory, and the State of Franklin ceased to exist. Tennessee became the sixteenth state in 1796.

President Andrew Jackson moved to Tennessee as a young man. His home, the Hermitage, and his grave are near Nashville. Tennessee was also the home of Presidents James K. Polk and Andrew Johnson.

President Jackson signed the Indian Removal Act of 1830. This law forced the Cherokee and other Native American tribes to leave their homes in Georgia and Tennessee and move to the Indian Territory in Oklahoma. About one-fourth of the people died of sickness, exposure, and starvation on this forced march, called the Trail of Tears.

The region became the site of the TVA (Tennessee Valley Authority) in 1933. This huge federal project built several dams and power plants. The project helped navigation and flood control and created electrical power. The TVA also created many lakes now used for recreation.

Capital: Nashville
Nickname: The Volunteer State
Motto: Agriculture and Commerce
Major Cities: Chattanooga, Knoxville, Memphis, Nashville
Population: 5,431,000 (est.)
Area: 42,200 square miles, 34th largest
Major Industries: Agriculture, music
Famous Citizens: W.C. Handy, Davy Crockett, David Farragut
Flower: Iris
Tree: Tulip Poplar
Bird: Mockingbird

Music is an important part of Tennessee's heritage. Early popular styles of music included folk ballads, gospel music, and bluegrass music. Nashville's Grand Ole Opry has been the long-time home to country and western productions.

Memphis, Tennessee's largest city, is the home of the blues. W. C. Handy, born in Memphis, created this distinct style of music. Handy combined the sounds of ragtime, honky tonk, and the songs of slaves into the blues. Memphis was also the home to "the king of rock and roll," Elvis Presley. Each day, hundreds of fans visit his mansion, Graceland, and his grave. Memphis was the site of the assassination of Dr. Martin Luther King, Jr. It is now the home of the National Civil Rights Museum.

Name: _____ Date: _____

Questions for Consideration

1. What was the name of an early French trading post in Tennessee?

    _____

2. How did the British get control of the region?

    _____

3. What was the name of the state formed by settlers in the eastern part of the region?

    _____

4. What is the name of Andrew Jackson's home?

    _____

5. In what year did Tennessee become a state?

    _____

6. What do the initials "TVA" stand for?

    _____

7. What famous Nashville site is the home to country and western music?

    _____

8. Who was the creator of the blues style of music?

    _____

9. What is the name of Elvis Presley's mansion?

    _____

10. In what city was civil rights leader Dr. Martin Luther King, Jr., assassinated?

    _____

Activities

Topics for special reports:

The TVA
Davy Crockett
Grand Ole Opry
Andrew Jackson

Locate: On the map, put the number for each item in the proper location.

1. Kentucky
2. Memphis
3. Mississippi
4. Mississippi River
5. Nashville
6. North Carolina

TEXAS

Spanish explorers were the first Europeans to visit what is now Texas. Texas comes from *tejas,* a Spanish word for a group of local Native Americans. *Tejas* meant "friends" or "friendly."

Alsonso de Pineda sailed along the coastline and claimed the region for Spain in 1519. Other early explorers included de Vaca, de Soto, Coronado, and La Salle. Ysleta, located near El Paso, became the first European settlement in 1682. It was originally a Spanish mission for relocated Native Americans. Several of the later missions still survive and are popular attractions for visitors.

Mexico gained independence from Spain in 1821. With independence, Texas became a Mexican state. Stephen Austin received permission from the Mexican government for Americans to settle in the region. Austin led 300 families into the territory. Soon, more Americans than Mexicans lived in the region. Friction grew between the American settlers and the Mexican government. Texas declared its independence in 1836. The most famous battle of Texas's war for independence occurred at the Alamo, a former mission in San Antonio. Over 170 individuals, including Davy Crockett and Jim Bowie, died defending the Alamo against the men of Santa Anna, the Mexican general. The Texans lost that battle, but eventually won the war. Sam Houston served as commander of the Texas army. After the war, he served as the republic's president. When Texas became a state, Houston served as its governor and later as U.S. senator.

For nine years Texas was an independent republic until it became the twenty-eighth state in 1845. The Texas Republic's flag contained one star. The same banner became the state flag when Texas joined the union. The state's nickname "the Lone Star State" comes from the single star of its flag.

Texas seceded from the Union to join the Confederacy in 1861. Because of its distance from the main conflict, no major Civil War battles occurred in the state. It was readmitted to the Union in 1870.

Agriculture became the state's first industry. With the aid of irrigation, crops included cotton, sorghum, corn, and wheat. However, the largest part of the agricultural economy became, and remains, the cattle industry. Early in the state's history, cattle drives moved the herds from Texas to the north for processing and shipment to eastern markets. The arrival of the railroads made the long cattle drives unnecessary.

The Texas oil boom began in 1901. The discovery of oil near Beaumont began what became the state's leading industry. In addition to oil, the state also has large deposits of natural gas. Other major industries in the state include electrical equipment, chemicals, and airplane parts.

Dallas was the site of the assassination of President John F. Kennedy on November 22, 1963. Texan Lyndon B. Johnson then became the nation's thirty-sixth president.

Texas became an important part of the United States' space program. The Houston Space Center opened in 1964.

Capital: Austin
Nickname: The Lone Star State
Motto: Friendship
Major Cities: Austin, Dallas, El Paso, Houston, San Antonio
Population: 19,760,000 (est.)
Area: 266,800 square miles, second largest
Major Industries: Agriculture, petroleum
Famous Citizens: Lyndon Johnson, Audie Murphy, Carol Burnett
Flower: Bluebonnet
Tree: Pecan
Bird: Mockingbird

Name: _____ Date: _____

Questions for Consideration

1. What was the name of the first European settlement in Texas?

   _____

2. When did Texas become a Mexican state?

   _____

3. Who led the first major group of Americans into Texas?

   _____

4. What was the most famous battle in Texas's war for independence?

   _____

5. How long was Texas an independent republic?

   _____

6. Who served as Texas's first governor?

   _____

7. What is responsible for the largest part of Texas's agricultural economy?

   _____

8. When did the Texas oil boom begin?

   _____

9. What historic event occurred in Dallas on November 22, 1963?

   _____

10. What major center opened in Houston in 1964?

   _____

Activities

Topics for special reports:

The Alamo
Stephen Austin
Sam Houston
Houston Space Center
Lyndon B. Johnson

Locate: On the map, put the number for each item in the proper location.

1. Austin
2. Dallas-Fort Worth
3. Gulf of Mexico
4. Houston
5. Oklahoma
6. Rio Grande River

UTAH

About 140 million years ago, the land that is now Utah contained a major river. Dinosaurs roamed the region in the era known as the Jurassic period. Many of the dinosaurs died near the river. A scientist named Earl Douglass made a major discovery in 1909. Douglass discovered the remains of several dinosaurs including the Allosaurus, Brontosaurus, Stegosaurus, and seven other types. Douglass's discovery was the largest concentration of dinosaur bones in the world. In 1992, scientists discovered the bones of the largest known velociraptor. Today, visitors can see some of these bones at the Dinosaur National Monument near Vernal, Utah.

Members of a group known as the Desert Culture lived in the region about 11,000 years ago. Another group, the Anasazi, moved into the region about 2,000 years ago. The Desert Culture people were hunters and gatherers. The Anasazi used agriculture and established the first permanent settlements. Later tribes of Native Americans included the Gosiute, Navajos, Piautes, Shoshone, and Utes. The name *Utah* came from the name of the Ute tribe. *Eutaw* means "dwellers on the tops of mountains."

Utah is the site of the Great Salt Lake. It covers over 1,700 miles and is the largest lake west of the Mississippi River. Salt Lake is seven times as salty as the ocean; only the Dead Sea contains more salt. Much of the nation's salt supply comes from the Great Salt Lake.

The first Europeans to explore the region were Spanish. Juan Rivera led a trading expedition through the region in 1765. Two missionaries, Silvestre Escalante and Francisco Domingues explored the area in 1776. Settlement of the area began in the early 1800s. Fur trappers moved into the region. Both the towns of Ogden and Provo were named for early trappers. Other settlers moved into the region from the south on the Old Spanish Trail.

Brigham Young and his followers settled in the state in 1847. Young was the leader of the Mormons, a religious group. Other religious groups often persecuted the Mormons. To avoid persecution, members of the group moved from New York to Ohio, then to Illinois where they founded the town of Nauvoo. After a mob murdered two of their leaders, the group again migrated. This time they moved into Utah and established Salt Lake City.

In 1848, millions of grasshoppers attacked the crops. The grasshoppers would have destroyed the crops, causing starvation of the settlers; however, thousands of sea gulls arrived and ate the grasshoppers. The sea gull later became the state bird. A monument honoring the sea gull stands in Temple Square in Salt Lake City.

The two parts of the Transcontinental Railroad joined at Promontory Point in 1869. This meant that passengers and goods could travel across the entire nation.

Utah became the forty-fifth state in 1896.

The discovery of uranium in 1951 began another of the state's major industries.

Capital: Salt Lake City
Nickname: The Beehive State
Motto: Industry
Major Cities: Ogden, Provo, Salt Lake City
Population: 2,100,000 (est.)
Area: 84,900 square miles, 11th largest
Major Industries: Agriculture, mining, electronics
Famous Citizens: John Browning, Robert Redford, Brigham Young, the Osmond family
Flower: Sego Lily
Tree: Blue Spruce
Bird: Sea Gull

Name: _____ Date: _____

Questions for Consideration

1. During what period did dinosaurs live near a major river in Utah?

   _____

2. Who discovered the site of the world's largest concentration of dinosaur bones?

   _____

3. What body of water contains more salt than the Great Salt Lake?

   _____

4. What was the nationality of the first Europeans to explore the Utah region?

   _____

5. For whom were the towns of Ogden and Provo named?

   _____

6. Who led the Mormons into Utah?

   _____

7. What major Utah city did the Mormons establish?

   _____

8. What animal has a monument in its honor in Temple Square?

   _____

9. Where did the two parts of the Transcontinental Railroad meet?

   _____

10. What major discovery was made in Utah in 1951?

   _____

Activities

Topics for special reports:

The Jurassic Period
Great Salt Lake
The Mormons
Transcontinental Railroad
Brigham Young
Uranium

Locate: On the map, put the number for each item in the proper location.

1. Arizona
2. Colorado
3. Salt Lake City
4. Nevada
5. Provo
6. Wyoming

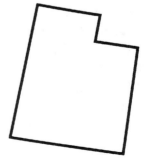

VERMONT

Native Americans hunted in this region for many centuries, but did not settle permanently until shortly before the arrival of the Europeans. Early explorers and settlers met members of the Algonquin and Iroquois who lived there.

French explorers were the first Europeans to visit and settle in what is now Vermont. The name *Vermont* comes from the French words meaning "green mountain."

Samuel de Champlain claimed the region for France in 1609. The French, British, and Americans all built forts in the area during the next several years. The French built Fort Ste. Anne in 1666 to protect their claim. The British came into the territory, and Captain Jacobus de Warm built a trading post in the region in 1690. Fort Drummer, built in 1749, was the first permanent European settlement.

The first canal built in the nation opened at Bellows Falls in 1802. This, the Lake Champlain Canal, and other canals aided in the early growth of the region's economy.

The British colonies of New York and New Hampshire both claimed the Vermont land. In 1771, the governor of New Hampshire sent a group of soldiers, the Green Mountain Boys, to remove New York settlers from Vermont.

During the Revolutionary War, the Green Mountain Boys, under the leadership of Ethan Allen, fought against the British. Their attack on Fort Ticonderoga in New York was a major American victory. After the Revolutionary War, Vermont remained independent. It took the name "New Connecticut" but soon changed its name to "The Republic of Vermont." As a republic, it had its own government and laws. It printed its own money and minted its own coins. It was the first government in America to ban slavery. Vermont remained an independent republic until it became the fourteenth state in 1791.

After the Revolutionary War, much of Vermont's trading was with Canada. Vermont became the center of smuggling during the War of 1812.

Vermont is the birthplace of two American presidents. Chester A. Arthur, born in Fairfield, became the twenty-first president in 1881. Calvin Coolidge became the thirtieth president in 1923. Coolidge was the vice president when President Warren G. Harding died. Coolidge's father was a justice of the peace. Shortly after midnight, on August 3, 1923, Coolidge's father gave him the oath of office.

Forests cover 75 percent of Vermont. Many of these trees contribute to the production of maple syrup. Vermont is the nation's leading producer of maple syrup. It produces over 400,000 gallons of syrup each year. Vermont is also a major supplier of marble and granite. The first marble quarry opened in East Dorset in 1785. The first granite quarry began production near Barre in 1815.

Vermont has become a tourist attraction in recent years. It is a major ski resort destination. The first ski resort opened at Woodstock in 1934. The state also has many scenic recreational areas.

Capital: Montpelier
Nickname: The Green Mountain State
Motto: Freedom and Unity
Major Cities: Burlington, Montpelier
Population: 591,000 (est.)
Area: 9,200 square miles, 43rd largest
Major Industries: Maple syrup, marble, granite, tourism
Famous Citizens: Ethan Allen, Chester Arthur, Calvin Coolidge
Flower: Red Clover
Tree: Sugar Maple
Bird: Hermit Thrush

Name: _____ Date: _____

Questions for Consideration

1. *Vermont* comes from French words meaning what?

   _____

2. What was the name of the first French fort built in the region in 1666?

   _____

3. Where was the nation's first canal located?

   _____

4. Who was the leader of the Green Mountain Boys?

   _____

5. What was the official title of Vermont from the end of the Revolutionary War until 1791?

   _____

6. What president's father gave him the oath of office?

   _____

7. How much of Vermont is covered by forests?

   _____

8. Vermont is the nation's leading supplier of what type of syrup?

   _____

9. Vermont is a major supplier of what two types of stone?

   _____

10. What was the name of Vermont's first ski resort?

   _____

Activities

Topics for special reports:

Ethan Allen
Chester A. Arthur
Calvin Coolidge
Maple Syrup
Marble or Granite

Locate: On the map, put the number for each item in the proper location.

1. Burlington
2. Canada
3. Lake Champlain
4. Montpelier
5. New Hampshire
6. New York

VIRGINIA

The first inhabitants of the land that is now Virginia arrived over 10,000 years ago. At the time of the arrival of the first Europeans, three major Native American groups, the Algonquin, Iroquois, and Sioux, lived in the region.

The first European settlement in Virginia was a Spanish mission built in 1570. The mission failed, and the Spanish abandoned it a short time later.

Virginia was named for Queen Elizabeth I of England. One of the Queen's nicknames was the "Virgin Queen."

English explorers visited the region in 1497. The first English colony was Jamestown, founded in 1607. According to legend, Pocahontas, the daughter of a Native American chief, saved the life of Jamestown founder Captain John Smith.

Jamestown, named for King James I of England, served as the colony's first capital. The government moved to Williamsburg in 1699. Today, Williamsburg has been restored to its appearance in the 1700s. It is the nation's most famous living museum.

Virginia was a leader in the Revolutionary War. Patrick Henry gave his famous "Give me liberty, or give me death" speech in the Williamsburg capitol. Many Revolutionary War battles occurred in the state. The British surrendered to the Americans at Yorktown in 1781. Virginia became the tenth state in 1788.

One of Virginia's nicknames is the "Mother of Presidents." The state is the birthplace of eight presidents. George Washington, Thomas Jefferson, James Madison, James Monroe, William Henry Harrison, John Tyler, Zachary Taylor, and Woodrow Wilson were all native Virginians. The homes of three of these are favorite visiting places for tourists. Washington's Mount Vernon, Jefferson's Monticello, and Madison's Montpelier attract thousands of visitors each year.

Virginia left the Union in 1861 to join the Confederacy. The western counties remained in favor of the Union. In 1861 they seceded from Virginia, and the western territory became the state of West Virginia in 1863.

The Union offered command of its army to Virginian Robert E. Lee. Instead, Lee chose to remain loyal to Virginia and lead the Confederate Army. Richmond soon became the capital of the Confederacy.

Over half of the Civil War battles were fought on Virginia soil. Major battles included Fredericksburg, Spotsylvania, Petersburg, and Manassas (also called Bull Run). The war ended with Lee's surrender to General Grant on April 9, 1865, at Appomattox Courthouse.

Agriculture has always been an important part of Virginia's economy. Tobacco became and remains the state's major crop. Today, other farm products include vegetables, cattle, chickens, and dairy products.

Manufacturing has increased steadily since the Civil War. Major Virginia industries include electronics, textiles, and plastics.

Mining industries in the state include coal, sandstone, and granite.

Capital: Richmond
Nickname: Old Dominion
Motto: Thus Always to Tyrants
Major Cities: Charlottesvile, Hampton Roads, Richmond
Population: 6,791,000 (est.)
Area: 40,800 square miles, 36th largest
Major Industries: Agriculture, chemicals, mining
Famous Citizens: (in addition to eight presidents) Robert E. Lee
Flower: Dogwood
Tree: American Dogwood
Bird: Cardinal

Name: _____ Date: _____

Questions for Consideration

1. For whom was Virginia named?

   _____

2. According to legend, who saved the life of Captain John Smith?

   _____

3. What Virginia city was restored to its 1700s appearance?

   _____

4. Who first said, "Give me liberty or give me death"?

   _____

5. How many presidents were born in Virginia?

   _____

6. What is the name of James Madison's home?

   _____

7. What city became the capital of the Confederacy?

   _____

8. How many Civil War battles happened on Virginia soil?

   _____

9. Where did Lee surrender to Grant?

   _____

10. What is Virginia's major agricultural crop?

   _____

Activities

Topics for special reports:

Robert E. Lee
Patrick Henry
Captain John Smith
Monticello
Mount Vernon
Williamsburg

Locate: On the map, put the number for each item in the proper location.

1. Atlantic Ocean
2. Appalachian Mountains
3. North Carolina
4. Richmond
5. Washington, D.C.
6. Williamsburg

WASHINGTON

Washington, named for George Washington, is the only state named for a president. The Cascade Mountain Range divides the state. The Cascades block much of the cloud cover from reaching the eastern part of the state. Because of this, western Washington is often wet and rainy, while the eastern region is much drier.

Most likely, the first European explorer to visit the Washington region was Bruno Heceta in 1775. Heceta claimed the region for Spain. The earliest English explorers included Captain James Cook in 1778 and George Vancouver who surveyed part of the region in 1792. In the same year, Robert Gray was the first American to explore the area. The Lewis and Clark Expedition of 1805–1806 was looking for a waterway from the middle of the country to the Pacific Ocean. They explored much of the Columbia River.

Fur traders and missionaries soon moved into the region. The North West Company established a trading post in 1810. The first permanent settlement was Fort Okanogan, built in 1811. Marcus Whitman founded a mission near present-day Walla Walla in 1836. In 1846, a treaty between the United States and Great Britain established the permanent border between Washington and Canada. Settlement of the region was slow until gold was discovered in 1855. The arrival of the railroads in 1883 also encouraged faster settlement. Washington became the forty-second state in 1889.

Seattle hosted the 1962 World's Fair. The most famous structure on the fairgrounds, the space needle, remains a symbol of the city. Other buildings from the fair now serve as theaters, a science museum, and a sports stadium. Spokane held the World's Fair, Expo '74, in 1974.

Washington contains many forests and recreation areas. National forests and park lands cover over two-thirds of the state. Almost 22 million acres of the state contain forests. The lumber and paper industries have long been important to the state's economy. The state contains six national parks and recreation areas, six national forests, 83 state parks, and over 8,000 rivers and lakes.

Some of the Cascade Mountains are in Washington. Mount Rainier, 14,411 feet above sea level, is the state's highest point. Mt. Rainier, Mt. Baker, and some other peaks still have glaciers. The mountains are dormant volcanoes. Mount St. Helens had a spectacular eruption in 1980. The explosion blew off over 1,300 feet of the mountain's top. Mount St. Helens is now a national monument.

The Grand Coulee Dam, completed in 1942, is the nation's largest producer of hydroelectric power. The dam also aided in farm irrigation. Over half a million acres of land became productive due to this irrigation. Aluminum production is one of the state's major industries. The production requires large amounts of electricity. Hydroelectric dams produce most of the needed power. The aircraft industry is also of great importance. The industry came to the region to be near the supply of electricity.

Capital: Olympia
Nickname: Evergreen State
Motto: By and By
Major Cities: Olympia, Seattle, Spokane, Tacoma
Population: 5,689,000 (est.)
Area: 66,600 square miles, 20th largest
Major Industries: Aircraft, aluminum, lumber
Famous Citizens: William Boeing, Bill Gates, Bing Crosby
Flower: Coast Rhododendron
Tree: Western Hemlock
Bird: Willow Goldfinch

Name: _____ Date: _____

Questions for Consideration

1. What mountain range divides Washington?

   _____

2. Who was the earliest English explorer to visit Washington?

   _____

3. What expedition explored the region in 1805–1806?

   _____

4. What important discovery occurred in Washington in 1855?

   _____

5. What two Washington cities hosted world's fairs?

   _____

6. What is the highest elevation in Washington?

   _____

7. What Washington mountain erupted in 1980?

   _____

8. What dam is the nation's largest producer of hydroelectric power?

   _____

9. The manufacturing of what Washington product requires large amounts of electricity?

   _____

10. Why did the aircraft industry locate in Washington?

   _____

Activities

Topics for special reports:

Aluminum
World's Fairs
Hydroelectric Power
National Forests

Locate: On the map, put the number for each item in the proper location.

1. Canada
2. Idaho
3. Oregon
4. Pacific Ocean
5. Seattle
6. Spokane
7. Olympia

WEST VIRGINIA

West Virginia entered the Union as part of the state of Virginia. It was not until the Civil War that it became a separate state. The earliest native inhabitants of the region that later became West Virginia used the area as hunting grounds. None of them established permanent settlements.

King James I of England granted the region to English settlers in 1609. It was not until 60 years later that the first English explorers entered the territory. The first permanent settlers did not arrive until 1726. Soon groups of pioneers looking for religious freedom established settlements including Mecklenburg (now named Shepherdstown).

Friction grew between settlers and the Native Americans. King George III signed a decree forbidding any settlement of the area until the settlers made peace treaties with the Native Americans. Many German, Dutch, Scotch-Irish, and other settlers ignored the King's order.

The Allegheny Mountains separate Virginia from West Virginia. The cultures of the two regions grew apart. The Virginia area depended on trade from the Atlantic Ocean coast. The West Virginia trade areas included the Ohio and Mississippi River Valleys. The Virginia farmers supported slavery, while the West Virginia farmers did not.

The last battle of the Revolutionary War occurred at Wheeling in 1782, when the colonists defeated a British and Indian attack on Fort Henry. At that time, the West Virginia settlers petitioned the Continental Congress for their own government. The Congress declined the request, and the entire region entered the Union as the state of Virginia.

George Washington chose Harper's Ferry as a U.S. arsenal in 1796. Abolitionist John Brown seized the arsenal in 1859. U.S. soldiers, under the command of Robert E. Lee, recaptured it. The government found Brown guilty of murder and treason and executed him. These events caused tensions that led to the Civil War. Virginia left the Union to join the Confederacy in 1861. The western counties then seceded from Virginia and formed an independent state they named Kanawha. They soon changed the name to West Virginia and petitioned to join the Union. West Virginia became the thirty-fifth state in 1863.

Miners first discovered coal in West Virginia in 1742. Coal soon became the region's major industry. Coal mining was a difficult job. Several reformers tried to improve the working conditions in the mines. The West Virginia chapter of the United Mine Workers began in 1890. During the 1920s violence often broke out as the miners tried to unionize. Mining was a dangerous occupation. Many mines collapsed or had fires and explosions. Notable disasters occurred quite often. The worst explosion occurred in 1907 at a mine near Nonogah, where 361 people were killed.

Decreasing demand for coal after World War II caused a depression in the region. The decline of the coal industry caused a reliance on other natural resources of the region including petroleum, natural gas, clay, gravel, and salt. Today, West Virginia relies on other industries including chemicals, metal products, and tourism and recreation to aid its economy.

Capital: Charleston
Nickname: Mountain State
Motto: Mountaineers are Always Free
Major Cities: Charleston, Wheeling, Huntington, Morgantown
Population: 1,811,000 (est.)
Area: 24,200 square miles, 41st largest
Major Industries: Coal mining, tourism, chemicals
Famous Citizens: Pearl Buck, Chuck Yeager, "Stonewall" Jackson
Flower: Rhododendron
Tree: Sugar Maple
Bird: Cardinal

Name: _____ Date: _____

Questions for Consideration

1. Who granted permission for settlers to move into West Virginia?

   _____

2. Who signed a decree forbidding the settlement of West Virginia?

   _____

3. What mountains separate West Virginia from Virginia?

   _____

4. What were West Virginia's trade areas?

   _____

5. Who seized the arsenal at Harper's Ferry in 1859?

   _____

6. During what war did West Virginia become a state?

   _____

7. When was coal discovered in West Virginia?

   _____

8. When did the West Virginia chapter of the United Mine Workers begin?

   _____

9. Near what West Virginia town did the state's worst mine disaster happen?

   _____

10. What caused a depression in West Virginia after World War II?

   _____

Activities

Topics for special reports:

Allegheny Mountains
John Brown
Pearl Buck
Coal Mining
United Mine Workers

Locate: On the map, put the number for each item in the proper location.

1. Charleston
2. Kentucky
3. Ohio
4. Pennsylvania
5. Virginia
6. Wheeling
7. Maryland

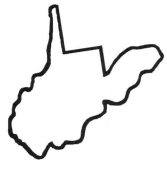

WISCONSIN

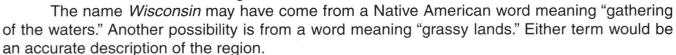

Humans have inhabited the Wisconsin region for over 14,000 years. The earliest inhabitants arrived soon after the last ice age. Other early cultures included the Old Copper Indians and the Mound Builders. A famous effigy mound in the shape of a bird remains near Madison.

Native American tribes living in the region when the first Europeans arrived included the Fox, Huron, Illinois, Ojibwa, Potawatomi, Sioux, and Winnebago.

The name *Wisconsin* may have come from a Native American word meaning "gathering of the waters." Another possibility is from a word meaning "grassy lands." Either term would be an accurate description of the region.

Wisconsin contains many bodies of water. It has over 10,000 streams and 8,700 lakes. Two of the Great Lakes, Michigan and Superior, border the state.

The grassy lands of the state supported early agriculture. Wisconsin was a major producer of wheat from the 1840s until after the Civil War. After the spread of wheat diseases, many farmers began raising dairy cattle. Since 1919, the state has been the nation's leader in the production of milk and milk products. Today, Wisconsin produces 40 percent of the nation's cheese and 20 percent of its butter.

Frenchman Jean Nicolet was the first European to explore the region. He visited in 1634 while trying to find a passage to China. Other French explorers, missionaries, and fur trappers soon moved into the region. The French gave control of the area to the British in 1763. The region came under the control of the United States in 1783. However, British troops remained until 1816. Before becoming the Wisconsin Territory, the region was part of three other territories. It was part of the Indiana Territory, then the Illinois Territory, and finally the Michigan Territory. Wisconsin became the thirtieth state in 1848.

The Ringling Brothers began their famous circus in their hometown of Baraboo in 1884. The Ringling circus joined with the Barnum & Bailey circus to form "The Greatest Show on Earth." Today, Baraboo is the location of a circus museum.

Wisconsin is the home to many firsts. Many historians believe it is the home of the Republican Party. A group met in Ripon to discuss their unhappiness with the political parties of their day, and they formed the Republican Party.

Margarethe Schurz started the first kindergarten in 1856. She based her ideas on German schools. *Kindergarten* means "children's garden" in German.

Though Wisconsin is famous for its dairy products, it also is the nation's leading producer of ginseng, beets, peas, and snap beans. It is the home to many industries also. It is home to major food processors and manufacturers of machinery, paper products, and electrical equipment.

The state became a major transportation center when the St. Lawrence Seaway opened in 1959. The Seaway opened Wisconsin ports on the Great Lakes to traffic to the Atlantic Ocean.

Capital: Madison
Nickname: The Badger State
Motto: Forward
Major Cities: Green Bay, Madison, Milwaukee, Racine
Population: 5,224,000 (est.)
Area: 56,100 square miles, 26th largest
Major Industry: Dairy products
Famous Citizens: Thornton Wilder, Spencer Tracy, Edna Ferber, Harry Houdini
Flower: Wood Violet
Tree: Sugar Maple
Bird: Robin

Name: _____ Date: _____

Questions for Consideration

1. What are the two possible meanings of *Wisconsin* mentioned in the narration?

   _____

2. What two Great Lakes border Wisconsin?

   _____

3. How much of the nation's cheese is from Wisconsin?

   _____

4. Who was the first European to explore the Wisconsin region?

   _____

5. What nation gained control of the region in 1763?

   _____

6. How many territories was Wisconsin part of before it became its own territory?

   _____

7. What famous circus began in Wisconsin?

   _____

8. What political party may have begun in Wisconsin?

   _____

9. What does *kindergarten* mean in German?

   _____

10. What enabled Wisconsin's ports to ship to the Atlantic Ocean?

    _____

Activities

Topics for special reports:

Cheese
Circus
Effigy Mounds
The Great Lakes
The Republican Party
St. Lawrence Seaway

Locate: On the map, put the number for each item in the proper location.

1. Illinois
2. Iowa
3. Lake Michigan
4. Lake Superior
5. Madison
6. Milwaukee

WYOMING

We know little about the first humans to live in the Wyoming region. Later tribes included Arapaho, Blackfoot, Cheyenne, Crow, Flathead, Sioux, and Ute. The name *Wyoming* came from a Delaware Native American word meaning "upon the great plain." The name of Wyoming's capital, Cheyenne, comes from one of the state's native tribes.

French fur traders may have been the first Europeans to visit the region in the 1700s. In 1805, François Antinon Larocque began trading with the natives. Just two years later, John Colter discovered geysers that are now part of Yellowstone National Park. John Frémont and Kit Carson explored the region in 1842.

Wyoming came under U.S. control as part of the Louisiana Purchase. Settlement of the region was slow. Early pioneers passed through the state on their way to Utah, Oregon, and California. Few stayed because of the lack of good farm land. Eventually, with the arrival of the Union Pacific Railroad, pioneers began settlements. Many of Wyoming's early settlers became cattle and sheep ranchers.

Conflicts often arose between the settlers and the Native American tribes. The government built several forts to protect the settlers and those traveling on westward. Today, visitors can see the remains or reconstructions of Forts Bridger, Fetterman, Steele, and Kearny. The tribes and the U.S. Army waged war for 35 years. Sioux Chief Red Cloud signed a peace agreement in 1868, but differences between the United States and Native Americans still exist. In 1991, Black Hills tribes fought to protect some of their sacred sites from being turned into tourist attractions.

Wyoming became the forty-fourth state in 1890. Wyoming was part of the "Wild West." Each year it has several events honoring that part of its history. Celebrations occur in Cheyenne, Cody, Jackson, and even the ghost town of South Pass City. Native Americans also continue to have powwows in several locations.

Wyoming has many natural wonders. Yellowstone became the first national park in 1872. The park contains the geyser "Old Faithful." Each hour, Old Faithful shoots a column of water over 100 feet into the air. Yellowstone also contains hundreds of species of plants and animals. Wyoming also has the first national monument, Devil's Tower, and the first national forest, Shoshone. Grand Teton National Park is another popular Wyoming attraction.

Capital: Cheyenne
Nickname: Equality State
Motto: Equal Rights
Major Cities: Casper, Cheyenne, Laramie
Population: 481,000 (est.)
Area: 98,000 square miles, 9th largest
Major Industries: Mining, agriculture, tourism
Famous Citizen: Buffalo Bill Cody
Flower: Indian Paintbrush
Tree: Cottonwood
Bird: Meadowlark

Wyoming's nickname is the "Equality State." In 1869, it became the first state to give voting privileges to women. The following year a 70-year-old grandmother, Eliza Swain, became the first woman to vote in a general election. Wyoming also had the first woman state senator, the first woman justice of the peace, and the first woman governor. It was also the first state to allow women to serve on juries.

Ranching remains an important part of the state's economy. In addition, Wyoming has many natural resources. Important discoveries include oil in 1833 and gold in 1842. More recent discoveries were uranium in 1951 and titanium in 1954.

Name: _____ Date: _____

Questions for Consideration

1. What does the name *Wyoming* mean?

   _____

2. Which major railroad helped bring settlement to Wyoming?

   _____

3. What Sioux chief signed a peace agreement in 1868?

   _____

4. What is the nation's most famous geyser?

   _____

5. What was the first national park?

   _____

6. What was the first national monument?

   _____

7. What was the first national forest?

   _____

8. What is Wyoming's nickname?

   _____

9. Who was Eliza Swain?

   _____

10. What was discovered in Wyoming in 1954?

    _____

Activities

Topics for special reports:

Kit Carson
Geysers
Voting Rights
Yellowstone National
    Park

Locate: On the map, put the number for each item in the proper location.

1. Casper
2. Cheyenne
3. Colorado
4. Idaho
5. Montana
6. Yellowstone Park

TERRITORIES

A **territory** is an area of land that is not part of a country, but is under the control of that country. Many of the states were territories or parts of territories before becoming states. For example, Wisconsin was part of three territories (the Indiana Territory, the Illinois Territory, and the Michigan Territory) before becoming the Wisconsin Territory. It was the Wisconsin Territory for 12 years before it became a state.

Several different relationships exist between a territory and its controlling country. Some territories are **possessions** of the governing country. The United States possesses and governs the Commonwealth of Puerto Rico, the Virgin Islands, Guam, and American Samoa.

Some territories are **trust territories**. The United States governed four Pacific Ocean units under the Trust Territory of the Pacific Islands established by the United Nations after World War II.

The relationships between the trust islands have changed during the last few years. The Mariana Islands, except Guam, are now a U.S. Commonwealth. The Marshall Islands and the Federated States of Micronesia are now independent states. They still have a "**free association**" with the Unites States. Palau accepted a special agreement of free association with the United States in 1993.

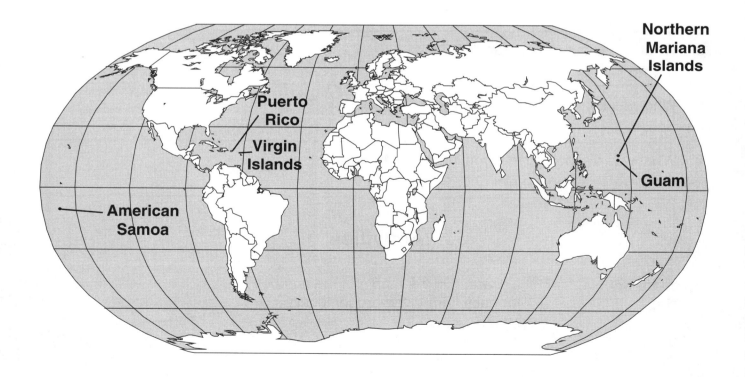

Name: _____ Date: _____

Questions for Consideration

1–2. Which two American territories are located in the Atlantic Ocean?

_____

3–5. Which three American territories are located in the Pacific Ocean?

_____

6–7. Which four territories are possessions of the United States?

_____

_____

8. Who established the Trust Territory of the Pacific Islands?

_____

9. Which former trust territory is now a commonwealth?

_____

10. Which territory established a free association agreement with the United States in 1993?

_____

Map Exercise

Locate the following on the map below: **American Samoa, Guam, Northern Mariana Islands, Puerto Rico, The Virgin Islands**

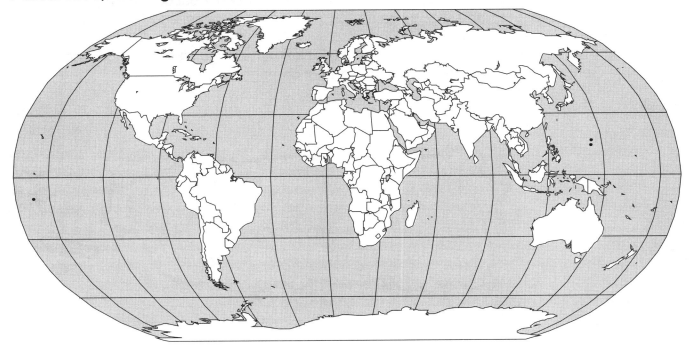

PUERTO RICO

The Commonwealth of Puerto Rico is the smallest of a group of islands known as the Greater Antilles in the Caribbean. The other islands of the Greater Antilles include Cuba, Jamaica, and Hispaniola (Dominican Republic and Haiti).

Puerto Rico is between the Atlantic Ocean to its north and the Caribbean Sea to its south. It is about 1,000 miles south and east of Florida.

The islands of Puerto Rico are the tops of a dormant volcano chain. The islands are mountainous and have over 700 miles of coastline. It has 3,435 square miles and includes the main island of Puerto Rico and the smaller islands of Mona, Vieques, and Culebra. The main island is 100 miles long and 35 miles wide.

Puerto Rico has a population of over 3,528,000. San Juan is its capital and largest city.

Columbus discovered Puerto Rico during his second voyage in 1493. Ponce de Leon explored the island in 1508 and referred to the region as *Puerto Rico* which, in Spanish, means "rich port." The Spanish later named the main island San Juan Bautista, and its capital Puerto Rico. During the Spanish control, many sugar plantations used West Indian and African slaves.

Puerto Rico remained under Spanish control until 1898. Spain surrendered it to the United States at the end of the Spanish-American War. The United States changed the name of the main island and the entire group of islands to Purto Rico in 1898 and Puerto Rico in 1932.

The island group became a U.S. territory in 1917. Its citizens became U.S. citizens at that time. It became a Commonwealth in 1952. It has local self-government, yet retains its affiliation with the United States. A resolution to ask for statehood failed by a narrow margin in 1998.

Puerto Rico has a mild climate. It has an average of only five cloudy days each year. It is a popular tourist destination, with over four million tourists, many on cruise liners, visiting the islands each year.

Sugar cane, coffee, and tobacco were Puerto Rico's major crops for many years. Recently, production of fruits, vegetables, and dairy products have replaced tobacco growing.

Ninety percent of Puerto Rico's exports go to the United States, and 75 percent of its imports come from there.

Many hurricanes reach Puerto Rico. In 1989, Hurricane Hugo hit the islands, and in 1998 Hurricane Gorges did over two billion dollars worth of damage to the islands.

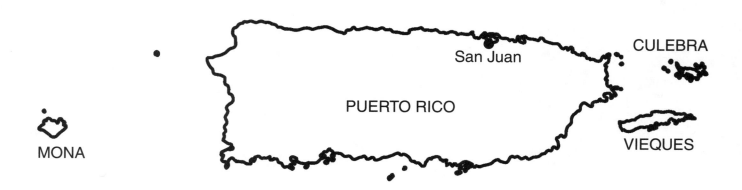

Name: _____ Date: _____

Questions for Consideration

1. Puerto Rico is the smallest of what group of islands?

   _____

2. Which state of the United States is closest to Puerto Rico?

   _____

3. How many islands make up Puerto Rico?

   _____

4. What is the name of the largest island?

   _____

5. What is the capital of Puerto Rico?

   _____

6. What European first discovered Puerto Rico?

   _____

7. What does *Puerto Rico* mean in Spanish?

   _____

8. When did Puerto Rico become a U.S. territory?

   _____

9. How many tourists visit Puerto Rico each year?

   _____

10. What two major hurricanes hit Puerto Rico in recent years?

    _____

THE VIRGIN ISLANDS

The Virgin Islands are in the Caribbean Sea about 60 miles east of Puerto Rico. Great Britain controls the northern and eastern islands. The United States controls three large islands: St. John, St. Croix, and St. Thomas, as well as 50 small islands. The U.S. islands have an area of about 136 square miles.

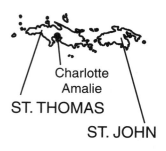

Charlotte
Amalie
ST. THOMAS
ST. JOHN

ST. CROIX

Christopher Columbus discovered the islands during his 1493 voyage. The islands then came under Spanish control. The English, Dutch, and French occupied St. Croix at various times. English buccaneers forced the Dutch out of the region. Danish settlers established a trading post in St. Thomas. Later, they claimed St. John and purchased St. Croix from France.

The United States bought the Virgin Islands from Denmark in 1917. The purchase gave the United States a base from which to protect the Panama Canal. The islanders became American citizens in 1927. They have their own governor and legislature.

Sugar cane and its products have long been a major industry of the islands. In recent years, tourism has grown into the major industry. Many large cruise ships visit the islands regularly.

Charlotte Amalie, on St. Thomas, is the capital of the islands. Other larger towns include Christiansted and Frederiksted on St. Croix.

GUAM

Guam is the largest of the Mariana Islands in the Pacific Ocean about 1,500 miles east of the Philippines. It is about 209 square miles.

Ferdinand Magellan discovered Guam in 1521. He named it "Island of Thieves" since natives took things from his ships. The Spanish controlled the island from 1565 to 1898.

The United States seized the island during the Spanish-American War in 1898. The United States then established a major naval base on the island. Today, the naval base covers about one-third of the island.

GUAM

The Japanese attacked and captured the island in 1941, but the United States recaptured the island in 1944.

Guam became a territory in 1950. Citizens of the island elected their own governor in 1970. In December 1999, the island's citizens voted on the form of government they wanted.

The island is a popular tourist site, especially for Japanese and Korean visitors.

Many typhoons reach Guam. Two typhoons, Keith and Paka, did major damage to the island in 1997.

Name: _____ Date: _____

Questions for Consideration

1. In what body of water are the Virgin Islands located?

   _____

2. Which three large islands of the Virgin Islands does the United States control?

   _____

3. What explorer first discovered the Virgin Islands?

   _____

4. From whom did the United States purchase the Virgin Islands?

   _____

5. What is the capital of the U.S. Virgin Islands?

   _____

6. In what body of water is Guam located?

   _____

7. What explorer first discovered Guam?

   _____

8. How much of Guam does the United States naval base cover?

   _____

9. What nation captured Guam in 1941?

   _____

10. When did Guam become a U.S. territory?

   _____

MINOR TERRITORIES

The United States has several small territories. **Navassa** is a tiny uninhabited island in the Caribbean between Jamaica and Haiti. The United States Coast Guard administers the island and uses it for a lighthouse.

The other small territories are in the Pacific Ocean. They are each less than four square miles. Some of the islands are transportation stopovers or military locations. Some are unoccupied or only occupied by U.S. military personnel and their workers. None of these territories have any industry or tourism.

Following is a list of minor territories with names that should be recognizable to students.

AMERICAN SAMOA - American Samoa is a group of six small islands in the Pacific Ocean. They are 2,300 miles southwest of Hawaii. The islands are Tutuila, Aunu'u, Ta'u, Olosega, Ofu, and Rose. The islands contain about seventy-seven square miles of land. The islands are the tops of volcanoes rising from the ocean floor.

The United States gained control of the islands in 1900. The islands are the only U.S. territory in the Southern Hemisphere.

American Samoa is an unincorporated territory. The people have their own system of chiefs and commonly-owned land. They are not U.S. citizens.

Exports include fish, coconuts, and handicrafts such as mats and baskets.

NORTHERN MARIANA ISLANDS - The Mariana Islands are in the Pacific Ocean about 1,500 miles east of the Philippines. The islands are the tops of volcanoes. Guam is the largest of the islands, but it is governed separately.

Ferdinand Magellan discovered the islands in 1521. Spain sold them to Germany in 1898. The Japanese gained control of the islands during World War I. The United States captured the islands in 1944 during World War II. The islands officially became part of the United States, and the people became U.S. citizens in 1986.

REPUBLIC OF PALAU - Palau consists of over 200 islands in the Pacific Ocean. The islands cover an area of 170 square miles of land. Palau is a United Nations trust territory administered by the United States. It accepted a special agreement of free association with the United States in 1993.

WAKE ISLAND - Wake Island is an atoll. An atoll is a coral reef surrounding a lagoon. The Japanese attacked Wake Island during World War II. U.S. Air Force personnel currently inhabit the island.

MIDWAY ISLANDS - Sand and Eastern Islands are coral islands. U.S. military personnel and their workers currently inhabit the islands.

JOHNSTON ATOLL - Johnston Atoll is 700 miles southwest of Hawaii. Government personnel and their workers inhabit the atoll.

PALMYRA ATOLL - A Hawaiian family currently owns Palmyra Atoll.

KINGMAN REEF - Kingman Reef is an abandoned reef.

HOWLAND, BAKER, and **JARVIS ISLANDS** - These three tiny islands near Hawaii are uninhabited.

Name: _____   Date: _____

Questions for Consideration

1. What tiny island between Jamaica and Haiti is the site of a lighthouse?

   _____

2. In what body of water is American Samoa located?

   _____

3. What is the only U.S. territory located in the Southern Hemisphere?

   _____

4. What explorer discovered the Mariana Islands?

   _____

5. When did the United States capture the Mariana Islands?

   _____

6. What territory is a United Nations trust territory administered by the United States?

   _____

7. What is an atoll?

   _____

8. Who attacked Wake Island during World War II?

   _____

9. Which U.S. territory is owned by a Hawaiian family?

   _____

10. Which U.S. territory is an abandoned reef?

    _____

Name: _____   Date: _____

MAP EXERCISES

THE NORTHEASTERN STATES

Using an atlas or encyclopedia to help, locate the following on the map provided on page 113.

STATES

CONNECTICUT	NEW JERSEY		
DELAWARE	NEW YORK		
MAINE	PENNSYLVANIA		
MARYLAND	RHODE ISLAND		
MASSACHUSETTS	VERMONT		
NEW HAMPSHIRE	WEST VIRGINIA		

CITIES

BALTIMORE	PHILADELPHIA
BOSTON	PORTLAND
CONCORD	PROVIDENCE
HARTFORD	TRENTON
MONTPELIER	WHEELING
NEW YORK CITY	WILMINGTON

GEOGRAPHIC FEATURES

ATLANTIC OCEAN	CANADA	CHESAPEAKE BAY	LAKE ERIE
LAKE ONTARIO	LONG ISLAND		

- -

MAP EXERCISES

THE SOUTHERN STATES

Using an atlas or encyclopedia to help, locate the following on the map provided on page 114.

STATES

ALABAMA	MISSISSIPPI
ARKANSAS	NORTH CAROLINA
FLORIDA	SOUTH CAROLINA
GEORGIA	TENNESSEE
LOUISIANA	VIRGINIA

CITIES

ATLANTA	MONTGOMERY
CHARLESTON	NASHVILLE
JACKSON	NEW ORLEANS
LITTLE ROCK	RALEIGH
MIAMI	RICHMOND

GEOGRAPHIC FEATURES

APPALACHIAN MOUNTAINS	ATLANTIC OCEAN	GULF OF MEXICO
MISSISSIPPI RIVER	OHIO RIVER	

Name: _____   Date: _____

MAP EXERCISES

THE MIDDLE STATES

Using an atlas or encyclopedia to help, locate the following on the map provided on page 115.

STATES

ILLINOIS	MISSOURI
INDIANA	NEBRASKA
IOWA	NORTH DAKOTA
KANSAS	OHIO
KENTUCKY	SOUTH DAKOTA
MICHIGAN	WISCONSIN
MINNESOTA	

CITIES

BISMARCK	LEXINGTON
CHICAGO	LINCOLN
COLUMBUS	MADISON
DES MOINES	MINNEAPOLIS / ST. PAUL
DETROIT	PIERRE
INDIANAPOLIS	SAINT LOUIS
KANSAS CITY	WICHITA

GEOGRAPHIC FEATURES

LAKE ERIE	LAKE HURON	LAKE MICHIGAN	LAKE SUPERIOR
MISSOURI RIVER	OHIO RIVER	MISSISSIPPI RIVER	

- -

MAP EXERCISES

THE SOUTHWESTERN STATES

Using an atlas or encyclopedia to help, locate the following on the map provided on page 116.

STATES

ARIZONA	NEW MEXICO
CALIFORNIA	OKLAHOMA
COLORADO	UTAH
HAWAII	TEXAS
NEVADA	

CITIES

ALBUQUERQUE	LOS ANGELES
DALLAS	OKLAHOMA CITY
DENVER	PHOENIX
HONOLULU	SALT LAKE CITY
HOUSTON	SAN FRANCISCO
LAS VEGAS	

GEOGRAPHIC FEATURES

COLORADO RIVER	GREAT SALT LAKE	MEXICO	PACIFIC OCEAN
RIO GRANDE			

Name: _____   Date: _____

MAP EXERCISES

THE NORTHWESTERN STATES

Using an atlas or encyclopedia to help, locate the following on the map provided on page 117.

STATES

ALASKA
IDAHO
MONTANA
OREGON
WASHINGTON
WYOMING

CITIES

ANCHORAGE	JACKSON
BARROW	JUNEAU
BILLINGS	PORTLAND
BOISE	SALEM
CHEYENNE	SEATTLE
HELENA	SPOKANE

GEOGRAPHIC FEATURES

ALEUTIAN ISLANDS	BITTERROOT MOUNTAIN RANGE
CANADA	CASCADE MOUNTAIN RANGE
COLUMBIA RIVER	PACIFIC OCEAN
SNAKE RIVER	PRINCE WILLIAM SOUND
YUKON RIVER	YELLOWSTONE NATIONAL PARK

Name: _____ Date: _____

THE NORTHEASTERN STATES MAP

Name: _____ Date: _____

THE SOUTHERN STATES MAP

Name: _____ Date: _____

THE MIDDLE STATES MAP

Name: _____ Date: _____

THE SOUTHWESTERN STATES MAP

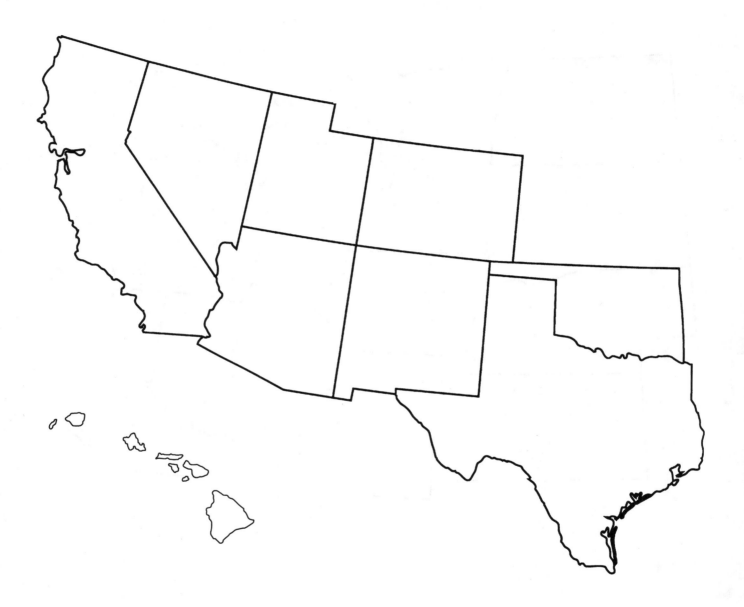

Name: _____   Date: _____

THE NORTHWESTERN STATES MAP

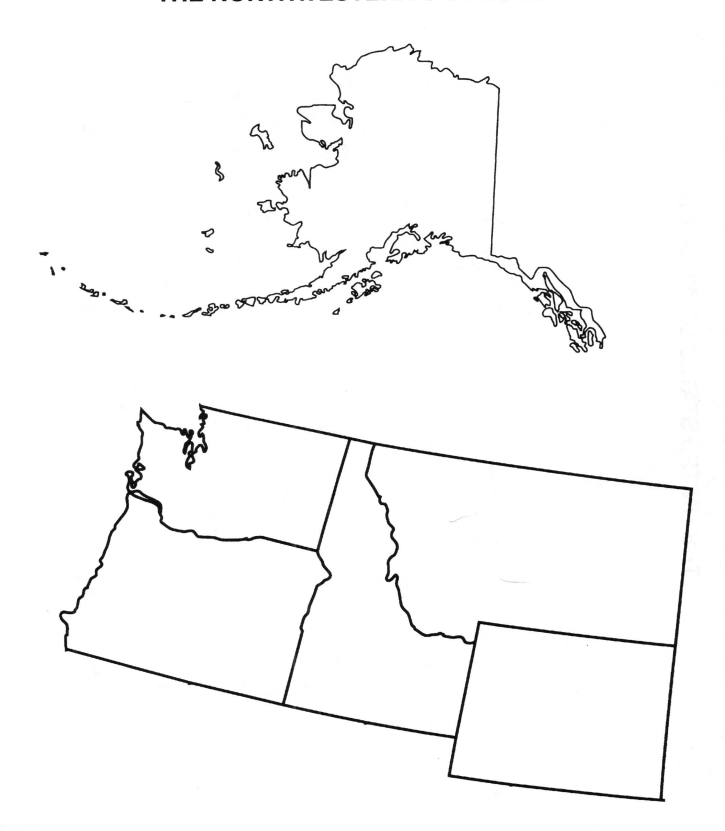

Name: _____ Date: _____

THE UNITED STATES OF AMERICA

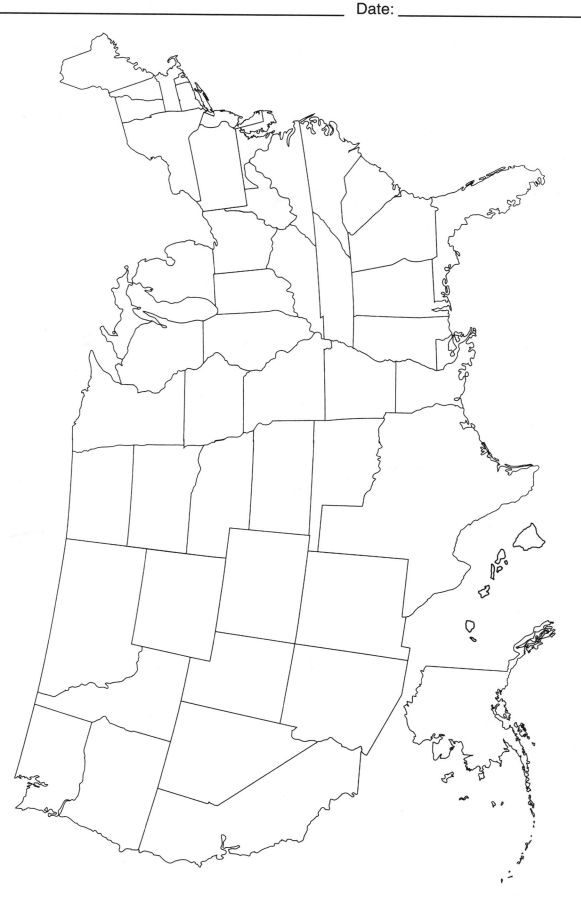

ANSWER KEYS

Alabama (page 3)
1. charcoal drawings
2. Hernando de Soto
3. the French
4. 1819
5. Montgomery
6. Annie Sullivan
7. boll weevil
8. George Washington Carver
9. Rosa Parks
10. Huntsville

Map:

Alaska (page 5)
1. "great land"
2. Alaska is twice the size of Texas.
3. the Last Frontier, Land of the Midnight Sun
4. -80°
5. northern lights
6. Danish
7. Russia
8. 1880
9. 1959
10. Trans-Alaska

Map:

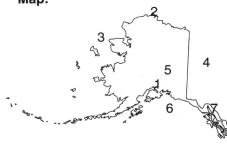

Arizona (page 7)
1. the Grand Canyon
2. Hoover Dam
3. 127°F
4. 23
5. Mexico
6. copper
7. Geronimo
8. gunfight at the O.K. Corral
9. Valentine's Day, 1912
10. Roosevelt Dam

Map:

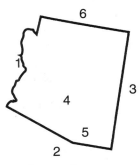

Arkansas (page 9)
1. 1906
2. aluminum
3. 47
4. Hernando de Soto
5. La Salle
6. Arkansas Post
7. the Louisiana Purchase
8. Pea Ridge, Prairie Grove
9. cotton
10. Wal-Mart

Map:

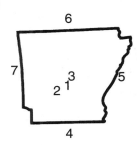

California (page 11)
1. Mt. Whitney
2. Death Valley
3. Yosemite Falls
4. redwoods
5. Hernando Cortés
6. 1848
7. Sutter's Mill
8. 1850
9. San Francisco
10. Richard Nixon

Map:

Colorado (page 13)
1. Pike's Peak
2. the Mile-High City
3. Royal Gorge
4. the Louisiana Purchase
5. Cherry Creek
6. the Matchless Mine
7. uranium
8. Colorado Springs
9. Aspen, Vail
10. "America the Beautiful"

Map:

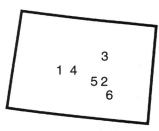

Connecticut (page 15)
1. the Fundamental Orders
2. King Charles II of England
3. in a hollow oak tree
4. "I regret that I have but one life to lose for my country."
5. a traitor
6. Mystic Seaport
7. USS *Nautilus*
8. Harriet Beecher Stowe
9. Winchester and Colt
10. insurance

Map:

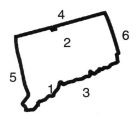

Delaware (page 17)
1. Henry Hudson
2. the Governor of Virginia, Lord de la War
3. Peter Minuit
4. Swedish pioneers
5. Pennsylvania
6. Blue Hen's Chickens
7. Caesar Rodney
8. gunpowder
9. chemical

10. It passed tax laws that gave advantages to corporations.

Map:

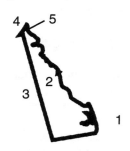

Florida (page 19)
1. Ponce de León
2. It is surrounded by water on three sides.
3. the Everglades
4. St. Augustine
5. 1819
6. the Seminoles
7. Cape Canaveral Space Center
8. orange
9. the Disney complex
10. Andrew

Map:

Georgia (page 21)
1. Hernando de Soto
2. King George II of England
3. Dahlonega
4. the Trail of Tears
5. 1861
6. the boll weevil
7. Atlanta
8. Franklin D. Roosevelt
9. James Earl Carter, Jr.
10. Dr. Martin Luther King, Jr.

Map:

Hawaii (page 23)
1. the Aloha State
2. 135
3. Oahu
4. eight
5. Polynesians
6. Captain James Cook
7. 1959
8. the attack on Pearl Harbor
9. USS *Arizona*
10. pineapples, sugar

Map:

Idaho (page 25)
1. potatoes
2. the Snake River
3. the members of the Lewis and Clark Expedition
4. the Nez Perce
5. fur traders
6. the Oregon Trail
7. the Gem State
8. 42
9. 3,200
10. 11

Map:

Illinois (page 27)
1. New Salem
2. Ronald Reagan
3. Joliet, Marquette
4. over 10,000
5. 1818
6. the Erie Canal
7. the Chicago Fire
8. the Sears Tower
9. the electric light (also the Ferris wheel)
10. corn, soybeans, cattle, hogs

Map:

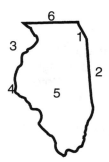

Indiana (page 29)
1. Kickapoo, Miami, Potawatomi, or Wea
2. La Salle and his men
3. George Rogers Clark
4. 1816
5. William Henry and Benjamin Harrison
6. Abraham Lincoln
7. agriculture
8. limestone
9. Studebaker
10. the Indianapolis 500

Map:

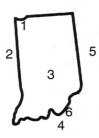

Iowa (page 31)
1. glaciers
2. "beautiful land"
3. Chief Black Hawk
4. Marquette and Joliet
5. the Spirit Lake Massacre
6. the Underground Railroad
7. Herbert Hoover
8. hogs
9. corn
10. the Missouri and Mississippi River flood

Map:

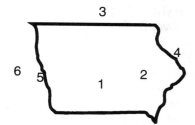

Kansas (page 33)
1. Coronado and his men
2. France
3. the Pony Express
4. Bleeding Kansas
5. 1861
6. Dodge City
7. Dwight D. Eisenhower
8. Alf Landon, Robert Dole
9. the Bread Basket of America
10. the Dust Bowl

Map:

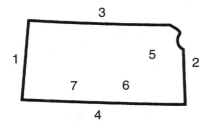

Kentucky (page 35)
1. the Bluegrass State
2. the Shawnee, the Cherokee
3. Cumberland Gap
4. Daniel Boone (other possibility: James Harrod)
5. 1792
6. Stephen Foster
7. Abraham Lincoln, Jefferson Davis
8. Fort Knox
9. the Kentucky Derby
10. Mammoth Cave

Map:

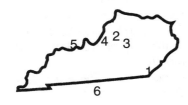

Louisiana (page 37)
1. Hernando de Soto
2. King Louis XIV of France
3. the French Quarter
4. Cajuns
5. Creoles
6. Andrew Jackson
7. 100 feet above sea level
8. Hurricane Katrina
9. Huey Long
10. oil

Map:

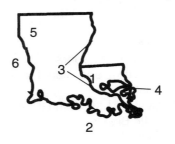

Maine (page 39)
1. about 1,100
2. over 80 percent
3. shipbuilding
4. Algonquin
5. Leif Ericson
6. the first naval battle
7. Missouri
8. 1842
9. paper manufacturing
10. lobster

Map:

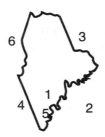

Maryland (page 41)
1. King Charles I of England
2. Queen Henrietta Maria, the wife of King Charles I of England
3. Lord Baltimore
4. Annapolis
5. to establish the nation's capital at Washington, D.C.
6. Francis Scott Key
7. Antietam
8. fishing and farming
9. it borders Washington, D.C.
10. Camp David

Map:

Massachusetts (page 43)
1. John Cabot
2. Pilgrims
3. Harvard
4. the Boston Tea Party
5. Paul Revere
6. George Bush
7. basketball
8. Emily Dickinson
9. textiles
10. the computer

Map:

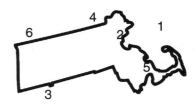

Michigan (page 45)
1. four
2. Upper Peninsula
3. the Mackinac Bridge
4. La Salle
5. the Erie Canal
6. R. E. Olds
7. Motown
8. John Harvey Kellogg
9. Post Toasties®
10. Gerald R. Ford

Map:

Minnesota (page 47)
1. over 10,000
2. Vikings
3. to protect the fur trade interests
4. 1858
5. "sky-colored water"
6. It is a major producer of wheat and dairy products.
7. mining
8. the St. Lawrence Seaway
9. across the Great Lakes
10. the Mississippi and other rivers flooded

Map:

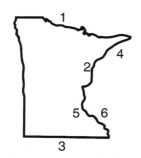

Mississippi (page 49)
1. Hernando de Soto
2. La Salle
3. as a fur trading post
4. 1787
5. the last home of Jefferson Davis
6. Vicksburg
7. cotton
8. James Meredith
9. Medgar Evers
10. Elvis Presley

Map:

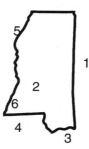

Missouri (page 51)
1. people of the long canoes
2. a French king
3. the arch, Jefferson National Expansion Memorial
4. Daniel Boone
5. Maine
6. the Pony Express
7. Jesse James
8. Mark Twain
9. Harry S Truman
10. Walt Disney

Map:

Montana (page 53)
1. the Treasure State
2. "mountain"
3. seven
4. French fur traders
5. the Lewis and Clark Expedition
6. 1860
7. Custer's Last Stand (Battle of the Little Big Horn)
8. Chief Joseph
9. Jeanette Rankin
10. Yellowstone National Park

Map:

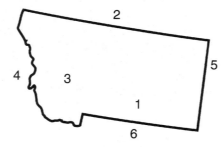

Nebraska (page 55)
1. the Great American Desert
2. La Salle
3. Lewis and Clark
4. Fort Atkinson
5. the Homestead Act
6. unicameral
7. corn
8. cattle and hogs
9. William Jennings Bryan
10. Father Edward Flanagan

Map:

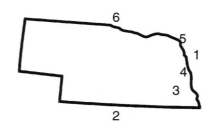

Nevada (page 57)
1. "snow covered"
2. Sierra Nevada
3. Father Francisco Garcés
4. John C. Frémont
5. Treaty of Guadelupe Hidalgo
6. the Comstock Lode
7. the Silver State
8. Hoover Dam
9. the MGM Grand
10. a testing site

Map:

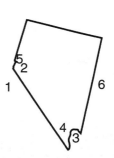

New Hampshire (page 59)
1. White Mountain Range (or Appalachian)
2. Mt. Washington
3. 231 miles per hour
4. Algonquins
5. *Bonhomme Richard*
6. Franklin Pierce
7. textiles
8. Treaty of Portsmouth
9. International Monetary Conference
10. the first presidential primary

Map:

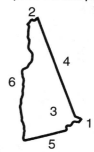

New Jersey (page 61)
1. the Garden State
2. the Lenni Lenape (or Algonquins)
3. Henry Hudson
4. Jersey, an English island
5. Battle of Trenton or Battle of Monmouth
6. Princeton and Trenton
7. Grover Cleveland
8. Woodrow Wilson
9. the first drive-in movie theater
10. Monopoly®

Map:

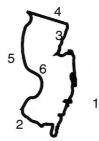

New Mexico (page 63)
1. tools
2. the Spanish
3. gold
4. San Juan Pueblo
5. Santa Fe
6. the Mexican War
7. a Mexican outlaw
8. copper, uranium
9. White Sands
10. Roswell

Map:

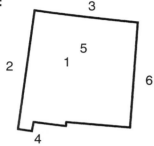

New York (page 65)
1. Algonquin and Iroquois
2. Henry Hudson
3. the Duke of York (brother of England's king)
4. 92
5. New York City
6. the Empire State
7. the Erie Canal
8. four
9. New Amsterdam
10. Al Qaeda

Map:

North Carolina (page 67)
1. King Charles I of England
2. Sir Walter Raleigh
3. Roanoke
4. Virginia Dare
5. Dolley Madison
6. Blackbeard
7. Battle of Moore's Creek Bridge
8. Kitty Hawk
9. Great Smoky Mountains National Park
10. cotton, tobacco

Map:

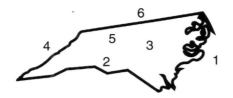

North Dakota (page 69)
1. because of the glaciers
2. Mandan
3. "allies" or "friends"
4. 1801
5. Fort Mandan
6. Sacajawea
7. bonanza
8. Benjamin Harrison
9. because of alphabetical order
10. oil

Map:

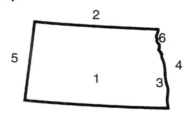

Ohio (page 71)
1. the Serpent Mound
2. "something great" or "great river"
3. the Mississippi River
4. Marietta
5. the Ohio and the Erie
6. a type of tree
7. seven
8. Dayton
9. B. F. Goodrich
10. John Glenn, Jr.

Map:

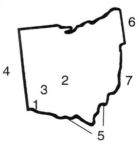

Oklahoma (page 73)
1. Clovis
2. "red man" or "land of red men"
3. the Trail of Tears
4. France and Spain

5. 160
6. sooners
7. *Oklahoma!*
8. the Dust Bowl
9. *The Grapes of Wrath*
10. 1995

Map:

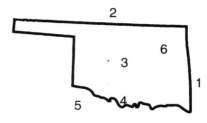

Oregon (page 75)
1. the Cascade Mountain Range
2. the Columbia River
3. Fort Clatsop
4. John Jacob Astor
5. 1841
6. 640 acres of land
7. discovery of gold
8. 1859
9. lumber
10. over 1,000

Map:

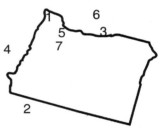

Pennsylvania (page 77)
1. Henry Hudson
2. "Penn's woods"
3. "city of brotherly love"
4. cattle and dairy products
5. Valley Forge
6. "Don't give up the ship."
7. an iron forge
8. near Titusville
9. the Battle of Gettysburg
10. Milton Hershey

Map:

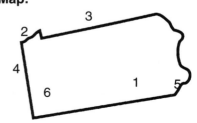

Rhode Island (page 79)
1. "red island"
2. Roger Williams
3. Providence
4. 1763
5. a ship
6. Newport
7. Nathanael Greene
8. a cotton mill
9. Rhode Island Red (a breed of chicken)
10. Newport
Map:

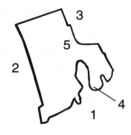

South Carolina (page 81)
1. Francisco Gordillo
2. King Charles I of England
3. Charles Towne
4. Blackbeard
5. the Palmetto State
6. Fort Sumter
7. blue dye
8. cotton
9. tobacco and soybeans
10. Myrtle Beach and Hilton Head Island
Map:

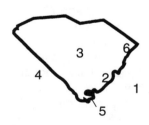

South Dakota (page 83)
1. "friends" or "allies"
2. Fort Pierre
3. North Dakota
4. Fort Buford
5. the Homestake Mine
6. uranium
7. a clay
8. Mount Rushmore
9. Chief Crazy Horse
10. Calamity Jane

Map:

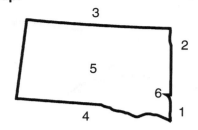

Tennessee (page 85)
1. French Lick
2. They won the French and Indian War.
3. the State of Franklin
4. the Hermitage
5. 1796
6. Tennessee Valley Authority
7. Grand Ole Opry
8. W. C. Handy
9. Graceland
10. Memphis
Map:

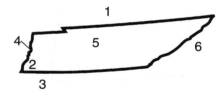

Texas (page 87)
1. Ysleta
2. 1821
3. Stephen Austin
4. the Battle of the Alamo
5. nine years
6. Sam Houston
7. cattle
8. 1901
9. the assassination of President John F. Kennedy
10. Houston Space Center
Map:

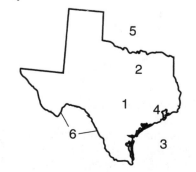

Utah (page 89)
1. Jurassic
2. Earl Douglass
3. the Dead Sea
4. Spanish
5. fur trappers
6. Brigham Young
7. Salt Lake City
8. sea gull
9. Promontory Point
10. uranium
Map:

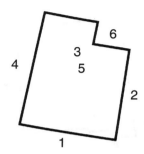

Vermont (page 91)
1. "green mountain"
2. Fort Ste. Anne
3. Bellows Falls
4. Ethan Allen
5. The Republic of Vermont
6. Calvin Coolidge
7. 75 percent
8. maple
9. granite, marble
10. Woodstock
Map:

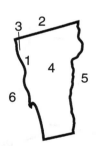

Virginia (page 93)
1. Queen Elizabeth I of England, the "Virgin Queen"
2. Pocahontas
3. Williamsburg
4. Patrick Henry
5. eight
6. Montpelier
7. Richmond
8. over half
9. Appomattox Courthouse
10. tobacco

Map:

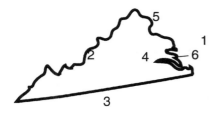

Washington (page 95)

1. the Cascades
2. Captain James Cook
3. Lewis and Clark Expedition
4. gold
5. Seattle, Spokane
6. Mt. Rainier (14,411 feet)
7. Mount St. Helens
8. Grand Coulee Dam
9. aluminum
10. to be near the supply of electricity

Map:

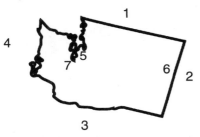

West Virginia (page 97)

1. King James I of England
2. King George III of England
3. Allegheny
4. Ohio and Mississippi River Valleys
5. John Brown
6. the Civil War
7. 1742
8. 1890
9. Nonogah
10. decreasing demand for coal

Map:

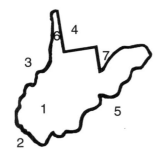

Wisconsin (page 99)

1. "gathering of waters" or "grassy lands"
2. Lake Michigan and Lake Superior
3. 40 percent
4. Jean Nicolet
5. Britain
6. three
7. Ringling Brothers (later Ringling, Barnum, and Bailey)
8. Republican
9. "children's garden"
10. the St. Lawrence Seaway

Map:

Wyoming (page 101)

1. "upon the great plain"
2. the Union Pacific
3. Red Cloud
4. Old Faithful
5. Yellowstone
6. Devil's Tower
7. Shoshone
8. the Equality State
9. the first woman to vote in a general election
10. titanium

Map:

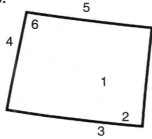

Territories (page 103)

1–2. Puerto Rico and the Virgin Islands
3–5. Guam, American Samoa, and the Northern Mariana Islands
6–7. Puerto Rico, the Virgin Islands, Guam, and American Samoa
8. the United Nations
9. The Mariana Islands (except Guam)

10. Palau

Map:

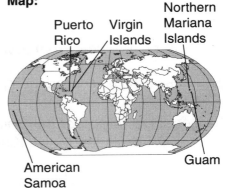

Puerto Rico (page 105)

1. the Greater Antilles
2. Florida
3. four
4. Puerto Rico
5. San Juan
6. Columbus
7. "rich port"
8. 1917
9. over four million
10. Hugo and Gorges

The Virgin Islands and Guam (page 107)

1. the Caribbean Sea
2. St. John, St. Croix, and St. Thomas
3. Christopher Columbus
4. Denmark
5. Charlotte Amalie
6. the Pacific Ocean
7. Ferdinand Magellan
8. about one-third
9. Japan
10. 1950

Minor Territories (page 109)

1. Navassa
2. the Pacific Ocean
3. American Samoa
4. Ferdinand Magellan
5. 1944 (during World War II)
6. Palau
7. a coral reef surrounding a lagoon
8. Japan
9. Palmyra Atoll
10. Kingman Reef

Region Maps (pages 113–117)

Teacher Check

BIBLIOGRAPHY

Aten, Jerry. *America: From Sea to Shining Sea.* Good Apple. 1988. (Grades 4 and up)

Aten, Jerry. *Fifty Nifty States.* Good Apple. 1990. (Grades 4 and up)

Bergen, Lara. *Discover the United States of America: State Stats, Fun Facts & a Puzzle of the 50 States.* Innovative Kids. 1999. (Grades 2–7)

Deltenre, Chantal and Martine Noblet. *The United States.* Carron's Educational Series, Inc. 1994. (Grades 5 and up)

_____ *Encyclopedia of the United States.* Scholastic, Inc. 1997.

Garrison, Edward T. *Short Stories about States & Capitals.* E. G. Photoprint Co. 1999. (Grades 5 and up)

Heinrichs, Ann. *America the Beautiful.* (set) Children's Press. 1998.

Hopkins, Lee Bennet. *These Great United States.* Simon & Schuster Children's. 2000.

Leedy, Loreen. *Celebrate the 50 States.* Holiday House, Inc. 1999.

Long, Cathryn J. *50 States.* Lowell House. 1999.

Miller, Millie and Cyndi Nelson. *The United States of America: A State-by-State Guide.* Scholastic, Inc. 1999.

Nikola-Lisa, W. *America: My Land, Your Land, Our Land.* Lee & Low Books, Inc. 1997.

Ross, Wilma S. *Fabulous Facts about the 50 States.* Demco Media, Ltd. 1986.

Sandak, Cass R. *The United States.* Silver Burdett Press (Crestwood House). 1994.

Schafer, Liza. *Fifty Great States.* Scholastic, Inc. 1993. (Grades 3–7)